William Perkins

William Perkins (1558–1602)
Portrait by Caffy Whitney

"The Wholesome Doctrine of the Gospel"

Faith and Love in the Writings of William Perkins

Introduced and Edited by
Andrew S. Ballitch and
J. Stephen Yuille

Reformation Heritage Books
Grand Rapids, Michigan

"The Wholesome Doctrine of the Gospel"
© 2020 by Andrew S. Ballitch and J. Stephen Yuille

All rights reserved. No part of this book may be used or reproduced in any manner whatsoever without written permission except in the case of brief quotations embodied in critical articles and reviews. Direct your requests to the publisher at the following addresses:

Reformation Heritage Books
2965 Leonard St. NE
Grand Rapids, MI 49525
616-977-0889
orders@heritagebooks.org
www.heritagebooks.org

Printed in the United States of America
20 21 22 23 24/10 9 8 7 6 5 4 3 2 1

Library of Congress Cataloging-in-Publication Data

Names: Perkins, William, 1558-1602, author. | Ballitch, Andrew S., editor.
Title: The wholesome doctrine of the Gospel : faith and love in the writings of William Perkins / introduced and edited by Andrew S. Ballitch and J. Stephen Yuille.
Description: Grand Rapids, Michigan : Reformation Heritgae Books, 2019. | Series: Profiles in reformed spirituality | Includes bibliographical references.
Identifiers: LCCN 2019012239 (print) | LCCN 2019013099 (ebook) | ISBN 9781601786821 (epub) | ISBN 9781601786814 (pbk. : alk. paper)
Subjects: LCSH: Perkins, William, 1558-1602. | Puritans. | Theology, Doctrinal—History—16th century. | Reformed Church—Doctrines—History—16th century.
Classification: LCC BX9339.P43 (ebook) | LCC BX9339.P43 A25 2019 (print) | DDC 230/.59092—dc23
LC record available at https://lccn.loc.gov/2019012239

For additional Reformed literature, request a free book list from Reformation Heritage Books at the above regular or e-mail address.

PROFILES IN REFORMED SPIRITUALITY
series editors—Joel R. Beeke and Michael A. G. Haykin

Other Books in the Series:

Michael Haykin, *"A Consuming Fire": The Piety of Alexander Whyte of Free St. George's*

Michael Haykin, *"A Sweet Flame": Piety in the Letters of Jonathan Edwards*

Michael Haykin and Steve Weaver, *"Devoted to the Service of the Temple": Piety, Persecution, and Ministry in the Writings of Hercules Collins*

Michael Haykin and Darrin R. Brooker, *"Christ Is All": The Piety of Horatius Bonar*

J. Stephen Yuille, *"Trading and Thriving in Godliness": The Piety of George Swinnock*

Joel R. Beeke, *"The Soul of Life": The Piety of John Calvin*

Thabiti Anyabwile, *"May We Meet in the Heavenly World": The Piety of Lemuel Haynes*

Joel R. Beeke and Mark Jones, *"A Habitual Sight of Him": The Christ-Centered Piety of Thomas Goodwin*

Matthew Vogan, *"The King in His Beauty": The Piety of Samuel Rutherford*

James M. Garretson, *"A Scribe Well-Trained": Archibald Alexander and the Life of Piety*

Roger D. Duke and Phil A. Newton, *"Venture All for God": Piety in the Writings of John Bunyan*

Adam Embry, *"An Honest, Well Experienced Heart": The Piety of John Flavel*

Ryan M. McGraw, *"The Foundation of Communion with God": The Trinitarian Piety of John Owen*

Dustin W. Benge, *"Sweetly Set on God": The Piety of David Brainerd*

Nathan A. Finn and Aaron Lumpkin, *"The Sum and Substance of the Gospel": The Christ-Centered Piety of Charles Haddon Spurgeon*

Table of Contents

Profiles in Reformed Spirituality ix
The Piety of William Perkins (1558–1602) xiii

Section One
Faith: Grounds of Doctrine to Be Believed

1. The Certainty of Scripture 3
2. The Sufficiency of Scripture 7
3. God's Holiness 13
4. God's Excellency 17
5. God Triune 21
6. God's Sovereignty 25
7. God's Mercy 29
8. The Supremacy of Christ 35
9. The Creation of Man 37
10. The Fall of Man 41
11. Law and Gospel 45
12. The Incarnation 49
13. Christ the Mediator 53
14. Faith 57
15. Justification 63
16. Regeneration 67
17. Christian Liberty 71
18. The Power of the Keys 75
19. The Church 79

20. The Resurrection 81
21. The Judgment........................ 85

Section Two
Love: Grounds of Doctrine to Be Practiced

22. Repentance........................... 91
23. Self-Denial 95
24. Choosing God 99
25. Fleeing Idolatry 103
26. Worshiping God......................107
27. Sanctifying God 113
28. Loving Our Neighbor..................117
29. Honoring Our Parents 121
30. Cultivating Virtue.....................125
31. Pursuing Our Calling..................129
32. Holding Faith........................133

Reading Perkins 137

Profiles in Reformed Spirituality

Charles Dickens's famous line in *A Tale of Two Cities*—"It was the best of times, it was the worst of times"—seems well suited to Western evangelicalism since the 1960s. On the one hand, these decades have seen much for which to praise God and to rejoice. In His goodness and grace, for instance, Reformed truth is no longer a house under siege. Growing numbers identify themselves theologically with what we hold to be biblical truth, namely, Reformed theology and piety. And yet, as an increasing number of Reformed authors have noted, there are many sectors of the surrounding western evangelicalism that are characterized by great shallowness and a trivialization of the weighty things of God. So much of evangelical worship seems barren. And when it comes to spirituality, there is little evidence of the riches of our heritage as Reformed evangelicals.

As it was at the time of the Reformation, when the watchword was *ad fontes*—"back to the sources"—so it is now: The way forward is backward. We need to go back to the spiritual heritage of Reformed evangelicalism to find the pathway forward. We cannot live in the past; to attempt to do so would be antiquarianism. But our Reformed forebearers in the faith can teach us much about Christianity, its doctrines, its passions, and its fruit.

And they can serve as our role models. As R. C. Sproul has noted of such giants as Augustine, Martin Luther, John Calvin, and Jonathan Edwards: "These men all were conquered, overwhelmed, and spiritually intoxicated by their vision of the holiness of God. Their minds and imaginations were captured by the majesty of God the Father. Each of them possessed a profound affection for the sweetness and excellence of Christ. There was in each of them a singular and unswerving loyalty to Christ that spoke of a citizenship in heaven that was always more precious to them than the applause of men."[1]

To be sure, we would not dream of placing these men and their writings alongside the Word of God. John Jewel (1522–1571), the Anglican apologist, once stated: "What say we of the fathers, Augustine, Ambrose, Jerome, Cyprian?... They were learned men, and learned fathers; the instruments of the mercy of God, and vessels full of grace. We despise them not, we read them, we reverence them, and give thanks unto God for them. Yet...we may not make them the foundation and warrant of our conscience: we may not put our trust in them. Our trust is in the name of the Lord."[2]

Seeking, then, both to honor the past and yet not idolize it, we are issuing these books in the series Profiles in Reformed Spirituality. The design is to introduce the spirituality and piety of the Reformed

---

1. R. C. Sproul, "An Invaluable Heritage," *Tabletalk* 23, no. 10 (October 1999): 5–6.

2. Cited in Barrington R. White, "Why Bother with History?," *Baptist History and Heritage* 4, no. 2 (July 1969): 85.

tradition by presenting descriptions of the lives of notable Christians with select passages from their works. This combination of biographical sketches and collected portions from primary sources gives a taste of the subjects' contributions to our spiritual heritage and some direction as to how the reader can find further edification through their works. It is the hope of the publisher that this series will provide riches for those areas where we are poor and light of day where we are stumbling in the deepening twilight.

—Joel R. Beeke
Michael A. G. Haykin

William Perkins

The Piety of William Perkins (1558–1602)

Coinciding with the years of Elizabeth I's illustrious reign (1558–1603) is the life of one of England's most influential theologians, William Perkins.[1] Scholars have described him as "the principal architect of Elizabethan Puritanism," "the Puritan theologian of Tudor times," "the most important Puritan writer," "the prince of Puritan theologians," "the most famous of all Puritan divines," and "the father of Puritanism." Some have gone so far as to include

---

1. For a brief account of Perkins's life, see *The Dictionary of National Biography*, ed. Sidney Lee (London: Smith, Elder, 1909). Also see Joel R. Beeke and Randall Pederson, *Meet the Puritans* (Grand Rapids: Reformation Heritage Books, 2006), 469–80; Ian Breward, ed., introduction to *The Works of William Perkins*, in *The Courtenay Library of Reformation Classics* (Appleford: Sutton Courtenay, 1970), 3:3–131; Benjamin Brook, *The Lives of the Puritans* (1813; repr., Morgan, Pa.: Soli Deo Gloria, 1996), 2:129–36; Charles Cooper and Thompson Cooper, *Athenae Cantabrigiensis 1586–1609* (Cambridge: Deighton, Bell, 1861), 2:335–41; Thomas Fuller, *Abel Redevivus: or, The Dead Yet Speaking: The Lives and Deaths of the Modern Divines* (London, 1651), 431–40; Thomas Fuller, *The Holy State* (Cambridge, 1642), 88–93; Samuel Clark, *The Marrow of Ecclesiastical History, Contained in the Lives of one hundred forty-eight Fathers, Schoolmen, First Reformers, and Modern Divines* (London, 1654), 850–53.

him—along with John Calvin and Theodore Beza—in "the trinity of the orthodox."[2]

Perkins's stature as an eminent theologian is noteworthy given his less than auspicious start in life.[3] He was born to Thomas and Hannah Perkins in the village of Marston Jabbet (near Coventry) in Bulkington Parish of Warwickshire. Very little is known of him until, at nineteen years of age, he enrolled at Christ's College, Cambridge. The university had been a major player in the English Reformation. From 1511 to 1514, Desiderius Erasmus lectured in Greek while preparing his translation of the New Testament. Within ten years, William Tyndale prepared his English translation from Erasmus's text. By the 1520s, Martin Luther's works were circulating among scholars. In 1534, Cambridge accepted Parliament's Act of Supremacy, thus recognizing the king as the head of the Church of England. And, in 1549, the divinity chair was offered to Martin

---

2. John Eusden, *Puritans, Lawyers, and Politics* (New Haven, Conn.: Yale University Press, 1958), 11; Paul Seaver, *The Puritan Lectureships: The Politics of Religious Dissent, 1560–1662* (Palo Alto, Calif.: Stanford University Press, 1970), 114; Christopher Hill, *God's Englishman: Oliver Cromwell and the English Revolution* (New York: Harper & Row, 1970), 38; J. I. Packer, *An Anglican to Remember: William Perkins: Puritan Populizer* (London: St. Antholin's Lectureship Charity, 1996), 1.

3. This introduction is adapted from Joel R. Beeke and J. Stephen Yuille, "Biographical Preface: William Perkins, the 'Father of Puritanism,'" in vol. 1 of *The Works of William Perkins* (Grand Rapids: Reformation Heritage Books, 2014), ix–xxxii.

Bucer, thereby demonstrating the success of the Cambridge reformers.[4]

It was at this decidedly *Protestant* institution where Perkins began his lifelong studies in 1577, entering Christ's College as a pensioner, suggesting that socially his family stood on the borderline of the gentry.[5] Perkins soon made a name for himself, but not for the reasons we might expect. "Quickly the wild fire of his youth began to break out," notes one biographer.[6] Another declares that he "was profane and prodigal, and addicted to drunkenness."[7] But Perkins eventually came under the godly influence of Laurence Chaderton (his personal tutor),[8] Richard Rogers, Richard Greenham, and others. More importantly, God began to work in Perkins's heart, producing deep conviction for sin. Benjamin Brook records a particularly noteworthy incident in which God brought Perkins face-to-face with his wretchedness: "As he was walking in the skirts of the town, he heard a woman say to a child that was forward

---

4. Harry Porter, *Reformation and Reaction in Tudor Cambridge* (Cambridge: Cambridge University Press, 1958), 51.

5. A *pensioner* paid the commons—that is, the common expenses of the college. A *sizar* was unable to pay the commons and, therefore, worked during his college career. A *scholar* was not required to pay the commons because the college waved his expenses due to his exceptional academic potential.

6. Fuller, *Abel Redevivus*, 432.

7. Cooper, *Athenae Cantabrigiensis*, 2:335.

8. Joel R. Beeke, "Laurence Chaderton: An Early Puritan Vision for Church and School," in *Church and School in Early Modern Protestantism: Studies in Honor of Richard A. Muller on the Maturation of a Theological Tradition*, ed. Jordan J. Ballor, David S. Sytsma, Jason Zuidema (Leiden: Brill, 2013), 321–37.

and peevish, 'Hold your tongue, or I will give you to drunken Perkins yonder.'"[9] The exact details of this story might be apocryphal, but the reality of Perkins's personal transformation was certainly real. Burdened with the weight of his sin, he turned to the Savior of sinners. Surrendering his wicked ways, he soon joined Chaderton, "the pope of Cambridge Puritanism,"[10] along with Rogers, Greenham, and others, in a spiritual brotherhood.

With renewed enthusiasm, Perkins devoted himself to his studies, receiving his bachelor's degree in 1581 and his master's degree in 1584. He was an industrious student. According to Thomas Fuller, "[Perkins] had a rare felicity in speedy reading of books, and as it were but turning them over would give an exact account of all considerables therein.... He took strict notice of all passages, as if he had dwelt on them particularly; perusing books so speedily, one would think he read nothing; so accurately, one would think he read all."[11]

Perkins's Ministry

At some point during his studies, Perkins began to preach on Sundays to the prisoners at Cambridge castle. Apparently, he pronounced "the word *damn* with such an emphasis as left a doleful echo in his

---

9. As found in Brook, *Lives of the Puritans*, 2:129; and Cooper, *Athenae Cantabrigiensis*, 2:335.

10. Patrick Collinson, *The Elizabethan Puritan Movement* (Berkeley: University of California Press, 1967), 125. See also Peter Lake, *Moderate Puritans and the Elizabethan Church* (Cambridge: Cambridge University Press, 1982).

11. Fuller, *Holy State*, 91.

auditors' ears a good while after."[12] Moreover, he applied "the terrors of the law so directly to the consciences of his hearers that their hearts would often sink under conviction."[13] His preaching was instrumental in delivering many from spiritual bondage. Samuel Clark tells of an occasion when Perkins confronted a condemned prisoner who was climbing the gallows, looking "half-dead."[14] Perkins said to the man: "What is the matter with you? Are you afraid of death?" The prisoner confessed that he was less afraid of death than of what would follow. Perkins responded, "Come down again, man, and you will see what God's grace will do to strengthen you." The prisoner complied. Kneeling together, Perkins offered "such an effectual prayer in confession of sins…as made the poor prisoner burst out into abundance of tears." Convinced the prisoner was brought "low enough, even to hell's gates," Perkins showed him the freeness of the gospel. Clark comments that the prisoner's eyes were opened "to see how the black lines of all his sins were crossed and cancelled with the red lines of his crucified Savior's precious blood; so graciously applying it to his wounded conscience, as made him break out into new showers of tears for joy of the inward consolation which he found." The prisoner climbed cheerfully up the ladder, testified of salvation in Christ's blood, and bore his death with patience, "as if he actually saw himself delivered from the hell which he feared before, and heaven

---

12. Clark, *Marrow of Ecclesiastical History*, 851.
13. Brook, *Lives of the Puritans*, 2:130.
14. Clark, *Marrow of Ecclesiastical History*, 852–53.

opened for the receiving of his soul, to the great rejoicing of the beholders."

Perkins's preaching soon attracted people from the town and university. As Fuller observes, "His sermons were not so plain but that the piously learned did admire them, nor so learned but that the plain did understand them."[15] Given his growing popularity as a preacher, Perkins was appointed in 1584 as lecturer at Great St. Andrew's Church, located across from Christ's College. From this pulpit, he reached people from all social classes, being "systematic, scholarly, solid, and simple."[16] The effectiveness of his preaching was due in large part to his penchant for casuistry—the art of dealing with "cases of conscience" through self-examination and scriptural application.[17] Each of his sermons "seemed all law and all gospel, all cordials and all corrosives, as the different necessities of people apprehended it."[18] Equally important, Perkins's personal godliness was a powerful example to all: "he lived his sermons, and as his preaching was a comment on his text, so his practice was a comment on his preaching."[19]

Around the time of his appointment to Great St. Andrew's, Perkins was also elected to a fellowship

---

15. Fuller, *Holy State*, 89–90.

16. Packer, *Anglican to Remember*, 3.

17. Ian Breward, "William Perkins and the Origins of Puritan Casuistry," *The Evangelist Quarterly* 40 (1968): 16–22; and George L. Mosse, *The Holy Pretence: A Study in Christianity and Reason of State from William Perkins to John Winthrop* (Oxford: Blackwell, 1957), 48–67.

18. Fuller, *Abel Redevivus*, 434.

19. Fuller, *Abel Redevivus*, 436.

The Piety of William Perkins

at Christ's College. He held this position from 1584 to 1595, serving as dean from 1590 to 1591. Fellows were responsible for preaching, lecturing, and tutoring students, acting as "guides to learning as well as guardians of finances, morals, and manners."[20] Perkins served the university in several additional capacities. He catechized students at Corpus Christi College on Thursday afternoons, lecturing on the Ten Commandments in a manner that deeply affected them.[21] He also worked as an adviser on Sunday afternoons, counseling the spiritually distressed. In these roles, Perkins influenced a generation of young students, including Richard Sibbes, John Cotton, John Preston, and William Ames. In the preface to one of his own works, Ames remarks, "I gladly call to mind the time, when being young, I heard worthy Master Perkins, so preach in a great assembly of students, that he instructed them soundly in the truth, stirred them up effectually to seek after godliness, made them fit for the kingdom of God; and by his own example showed them, what things they should chiefly intend, that they might promote true religion, in the power of it, unto God's glory, and others' salvation."[22]

While at Cambridge, Perkins engaged in several controversies. When Elizabeth ascended the throne

---

20. Mark Curtis, *Oxford and Cambridge in Transition 1558–1642* (Oxford: Oxford University Press, 1965), 80.

21. Gerald R. Bragg, *Freedom and Authority: A Study of English Thought in the Early Seventeenth Century* (Philadelphia: Westminster Press, 1975), 138.

22. William Ames, "To the Reader," in *Conscience with the Power and Cases thereof* (London, 1643), n.p.

in 1558, most of the English Protestants who had fled to the Continent during the reign of Mary returned to England. Some were discouraged with the state of the church, desiring to remove all remnants of Roman Catholicism. Some of them also desired to reform the church's government on the basis of Presbyterianism.[23] These men encompassed a broad spectrum of opinion, yet all shared one common denominator—dissatisfaction with the extent of the Reformation in England. As Neil Keeble notes, "The term 'Puritan' became current during the 1560s as a nickname for Protestants who, dissatisfied with the Elizabethan Settlement of the church by the Act of Uniformity of 1559, would have subscribed to the contention of the Admonition to Parliament of 1572 that 'we in England are so far off, from having a church rightly reformed, according to the prescript of God's Word, that as yet we are not come to the outward face of the same.'"[24]

Perkins never openly allied himself with the likes of Thomas Cartwright, an outspoken proponent of Presbyterianism. In 1591, he was called before the Star Chamber as a witness against the defendants Thomas Cartwright and Edmund Snape. Two years earlier, these three men, along with Laurence Chaderton, had been present at St. John's College for a

---

23. For an overview of the Admonition to Parliament in 1572, see Peter Lake, *Anglicans and Puritans? Presbyterianism and English Conformist Thought from Whitgift to Hooker* (London: Unwin Hyman, 1988).

24. Neil Keeble, "Puritan Spirituality," in *The Westminster Dictionary of Christian Spirituality*, ed. G. S. Wakefield (Philadelphia: Westminster Press, 1983), 323.

discussion concerning the Presbyterian Book of Discipline. While confirming the defendants' presence, Perkins testified that this was an isolated meeting, and that he was unaware of any talk of the actual implementation of presbyteries.[25] Perkins had even less sympathy for the separatist movement, commenting, "No man ought to sever himself from the Church of England, for some wants that be therein. We have the true doctrine of Christ preached among us by God's blessing, and though there be corruptions in manners among us, yea, and though they could justly find fault with our doctrine, yet so long as we hold Christ, no man ought to sever himself from our Church."[26] Like his mentor, Chaderton, Perkins worked to purify the established church rather than joining those who advocated separation. Instead of focusing his attention on church polity, he was primarily concerned with addressing pastoral inadequacies, spiritual deficiencies, and widespread ignorance within the church. That being said, Perkins occasionally expressed his dissatisfaction over the condition of the Church of England. On January 19, 1587, he was called before the vice-chancellor at Cambridge to give an account for a sermon in which he allegedly railed against "superstitious" and "antichristian" practices.[27] Among other things, he

---

25. W. B. Patterson, *William Perkins and the Making of Protestant England* (Oxford: Oxford University Press, 2014), 46–48.

26. William Perkins, *A Godly and Learned Exposition Upon Christ's Sermon in the Mount*, in *The Works of William Perkins* (London, 1631), 3:264.

27. Cooper, *Athenae Cantabrigiensis*, 2:335; and Brooks, *Lives of the Puritans*, 2:131.

objected to kneeling and facing east while receiving the Lord's Supper. Perkins denied some of the charges while modifying several of his comments. After this brush with the authorities, it appears he intentionally steered clear of such controversies.

In the 1590s, ecclesiastical concerns were overshadowed by more important theological questions regarding the nature of grace.[28] Peter Baro (Lady Margaret's professor of divinity) argued that God's work of predestination is based upon His foreknowledge of an individual's faith and works. Perkins responded with *A Golden Chain* (*Armilla Aurea*), in which he openly challenged Baro's position. "God's decree," writes Perkins, "in as much as it concerns man, is called predestination, which is the decree of God, by which He has ordained all men to a certain and everlasting estate, that is, either to salvation or condemnation, for His own glory."[29] For Perkins, God executes His decree through four "degrees": effectual calling, whereby "a sinner, being severed from the world, is entertained into God's family"; justification, whereby "such as believe, are accounted just before God through the obedience of Christ Jesus"; sanctification, whereby "such as believe, being delivered from the tyranny of sin,

---

28. For more on this controversy, see Mark Shaw, "William Perkins and the New Pelagians: Another Look at the Cambridge Predestination Controversy of the 1590s," *Westminster Theological Journal* 58 (1996): 267–301.

29. William Perkins, *A Golden Chain: or, the Description of Theology: Containing the Order of the Causes of Salvation and Damnation, According to God's Word*, in *The Works of William Perkins* (London, 1608), 1:16.

are by little and little renewed in holiness and righteousness"; and glorification, whereby the saints are perfectly transformed "into the image of the Son of God."[30] This "golden chain" constituted, for Perkins, the definitive word on God's grace.

During his time at Cambridge, Perkins earned an unrivaled reputation as a teacher and writer. John Cotton considered Perkins's ministry the "one good reason why there came so many excellent preachers out of Cambridge in England, more than out of Oxford."[31] When Thomas Goodwin enrolled at Cambridge in 1613, a full ten years after Perkins's death, he could write, "The town was then filled with the discourse of the power of Master Perkins's ministry, still fresh in most men's memories."[32]

In 1595, Perkins resigned his fellowship at Christ's College to marry a young widow, Timothye Cradock. During their seven years of marriage, they conceived seven children—three of whom died in infancy. He continued to preach at Great St. Andrew's Church until his death (caused by complications arising from kidney stones) in 1602 at age forty-four.[33] Expressing the sentiment of many throughout England, Perkins's closest friend, James Montagu, later bishop

---

30. Perkins, *Golden Chain*, 1:78–93.

31. Louis B. Wright, "William Perkins: Elizabethan Apostle of 'Practical Divinity,'" *Huntington Library Quarterly* 3 (1940): 194.

32. Thomas Goodwin as quoted in Breward, *Works of William Perkins*, 3:9.

33. Perkins was buried in the churchyard of Great St. Andrew's. Everett Emerson, *English Puritanism from John Hooper to John Milton* (Durham: Duke University Press, 1968), 159.

Thomas Goodwin (1600–1680)

A Puritan Congregationalist and member of the Westminster Assembly. Having enrolled at Cambridge ten years after Perkins's death, Goodwin remarked, "The town was then filled with the discourse of the power of Master Perkins's ministry, still fresh in most men's memories."

of Winchester, preached the funeral sermon from Joshua 1:2, saying, "Moses my servant is dead."

Perkins's influence as a theologian continued unabated after his death. This was due in large part to the widespread popularity of his writings. They include discourses on various cases of conscience; treatises on worship, preaching, assurance, predestination, the Apostles' Creed, the Lord's Prayer, and the errors of Roman Catholicism; and expositions of Galatians 1–5, Matthew 5–7, Hebrews 11, Jude, and Revelation 1–3. Eleven posthumous editions, containing nearly fifty books, were printed by 1635.[34] At least fifty editions of his works were printed in Germany and Switzerland. There were 185 seventeenth-century printings of his individual or collected works in Dutch,[35] twice as many as any other Puritan.[36] Perkins and his most influential student, William Ames, impacted numerous *Nadere Reformatie* (Dutch Further Reformation) theologians. His writings were also translated into Spanish, Welsh, Irish, French, Italian, Hungarian, and Czech.[37]

---

34. Harry Porter claims that Perkins wrote more than fifty of the 210 books printed in Cambridge between 1585 and 1618. *Reformation and Reaction*, 260–64.

35. J. Van der Haar, *From Abbadie to Young: A Bibliography of English, mostly Puritan Works, Translated i/o Dutch Language* (Veenendaal: Kool, 1980), 1:96–108.

36. Cornelis W. Schoneveld, *Intertraffic of the Mind: Studies in Seventeenth-Century Anglo-Dutch Translation with a Checklist of Books Translated from English into Dutch, 1600–1700* (Leiden: Brill, 1983), 220–26.

37. Munson, "William Perkins: Theologian of Transition," 56–59; and Wright, "William Perkins," 171.

In New England, close to one hundred Cambridge men, including William Brewster of Plymouth, Thomas Hooker of Connecticut, John Winthrop of Massachusetts Bay, and Roger Williams of Rhode Island, lived in Perkins's shadow. Richard Mather was converted while reading from Perkins, and—more than a century later—Jonathan Edwards was gleaning insights from Perkins's writings.[38] According to Samuel Morison, "a typical Plymouth Colony library comprised a large and a small Bible, [Henry] Ainsworth's translation of the Psalms, and the works of William Perkins, a favorite theologian."[39] Perry Miller observes, "Anyone who reads the writings of early New England learns that Perkins was indeed a towering figure in their eyes."[40]

Perkins's Theology

Perkins embraced what he described as Scripture's "infallible certainty," meaning "the testimony of Scripture is the testimony of God Himself."[41] Because Scripture is the very Word of God, Perkins viewed it as the means by which God reveals Himself and imparts grace to His people; and this necessarily implied that Scripture must stand alone at the center of the life of the Christian and the church.

Owing to his concept of Scripture's "infallible certainty," Perkins adopted the Bible as the axiom

---

38. Porter, *Reformation and Reaction*, 258–60.

39. Samuel Morison, *The Intellectual Life of Colonial New England*, 2nd ed. (New York: University Press, 1956), 134.

40. Perry Miller, *Errand into the Wilderness* (Cambridge: Belknap, 1956), 57–59.

41. Perkins, *Christ's Sermon in the Mount*, 3:219–26.

of all his thinking and the focus of all his teaching. To that end, he devised a very simple structure in preaching and writing: exposition, doctrines, reasons, and uses.[42] He was committed to this structure because he believed it was the best way to convince the judgment and embrace the affections, thereby bringing the mind into vital contact with the meaning of Scripture.

When it comes to his actual exposition of Scripture, Perkins practiced Christ-centered exegesis. This approach stemmed from his great desire and design to proclaim Christ above all else. As recorded in Luke 6:48, Christ describes the wise man as one who "built an house, and digged deep, and laid the foundation on a rock." Perkins viewed this statement as the archetype of true wisdom. To begin with, true wisdom consists of *digging deep*. For Perkins, this is the cultivation of conviction for sin. Without a "ransacking of the heart," we cannot lay a good foundation.[43] Second, true wisdom consists of *choosing a rock*. Our works of righteousness cannot provide any protection against God's judgment. We need to stand upon a secure rock, meaning we must look away from ourselves to Christ for salvation. Third, true wisdom consists of *laying a foundation*. According to

---

42. William Perkins, *Art of Prophesying; or, A treatise concerning the sacred and only true manner and method of preaching*, in *The Works of William Perkins* (London, 1631), 2:341. For more on Perkins's approach to biblical interpretation, see Andrew S. Ballitch, "Scripture is both the Glosse and the Text: Biblical Interpretation and its Implementation in the Works of William Perkins" (PhD diss., The Southern Baptist Theological Seminary, 2017).

43. Perkins, *Christ's Sermon in the Mount*, 3:256.

Perkins, "This is done by our faith in Christ: for as mutual love joins one man unto another, so true faith makes us one with Christ."[44]

By means of this union, "Christ, with all His benefits, is made ours."[45] In particular, we become the beneficiaries of justification. Perkins writes, "The form of justification, is, as it were, a kind of translation of the believer's sins unto Christ, and again Christ's righteousness unto the believer, by a reciprocal or mutual imputation."[46] This concept of "mutual imputation" flowed directly from Perkins's covenant theology.[47] In the garden, God established the covenant of works with Adam and his posterity. That is to say, Adam stood in the place of his descendants, and God gave him a specific commandment. When Adam sinned, God counted his sin as his posterity's sin, his guilt as his posterity's guilt, and his punishment as his posterity's punishment. This gave rise to the need for another covenant—the covenant of grace. Adam has a counterpart—the last Adam (Christ). Just as Adam's "offense" resulted in death and condemnation for his posterity, so too Christ's "gift by grace" resulted in life and justification for His posterity (Romans 5:15–19). For Perkins, when

---

44. Perkins, *Christ's Sermon in the Mount*, 3:256. R. Tudur Jones demonstrates that from Perkins to John Bunyan, the Puritans stress "union with Christ." He finds it present in earlier Protestantism; for example, Calvin insisted that there is no benefit unless the Holy Spirit engrafts us into Christ. "Union with Christ: The Existential Nerve of Puritan Piety," *Tyndale Bulletin* 41 (1990): 186–208.

45. Perkins, *Golden Chain*, 1:83.

46. Perkins, *Golden Chain*, 1:82.

47. Perkins, *Golden Chain*, 1:170.

we believe, we are no longer in Adam (under the covenant of works) because we have been united with Christ (under the covenant of grace), who has fulfilled the covenant of works on our behalf. This is the framework for Perkins's understanding of "mutual imputation"—Christ fulfills the covenant of works, meeting its requirement by His active obedience (life) and paying its penalty by His passive obedience (death).

Perkins, therefore, insisted that we are saved by virtue of union with Christ through faith. He insisted with equal vigor that saving faith includes far more than intellectual assent. According to Mark Shaw, Perkins's "covenant theology enabled him to follow a consistent line of co-action which gave strong emphasis to God's sovereign grace in Christ as the ultimate cause of salvation while at the same time emphasizing the necessity of human response.... The human psyche as created by God needed the sovereignty of grace to deliver it from the condemnation it was helpless to alter while at the same time it needed to apply and respond to his grace."[48] In other words, Perkins did not believe we are simply forced into a state of salvation without any awareness of our own experience. Instead, he affirmed that God proceeds with us by steps, so that we are involved in the process.

Perkins adhered wholeheartedly to God's sovereign grace in salvation. He believed that "man must be considered in a four-fold estate"—namely, as he is

---

48. Mark Shaw, "Drama in the Meeting House: The Concept of Conversion in the Theology of William Perkins," *Westminster Theological Journal* 45 (1983): 71.

"created," "corrupted," "renewed," and "glorified."[49] Before the fall, man's will possessed "liberty of nature, in which he could will either good or evil." After the fall, man's "liberty of nature" remained, meaning he still possesses the freedom to choose.[50] However, man's "liberty of nature" is now "joined with a necessity of sinning, because it stands in bondage under sin." Perkins believed that, in this estate, man's will is appropriately termed by Augustine, "the bound free-will."[51] That is to say, man's will is free in the actions it performs but captive in the way it performs them. In this condition, his heart is so captivated by sin that he has no power to escape from its bondage. For this reason, he stands in need of God's sovereign grace. Although Perkins preached about God's sovereign grace from eternity and God's covenant acts of salvation, he was particularly concerned about how this redemptive process breaks through into our experience. He wanted to explain how we respond to God's sovereign acts—that is, how the covenant of grace impacts us so as to move us from initial faith to full assurance.

Perkins's Piety

At this point, Perkins's experimental piety steps to the fore.[52] The term *experimental* comes from the

---

49. William Perkins, *A Reformed Catholic*, in *The Works of William Perkins* (London, 1608), 1:551.

50. William Perkins, *A Treatise of God's Free Grace, and Man's Free-Will*, in *The Works of William Perkins* (London, 1608), 1:709.

51. Perkins, *Treatise of God's Free Grace*, 1:703.

52. For more on this, see Joel R. Beeke, "The Lasting Power of Reformed Experiential Preaching," in *Feed My Sheep: A Passionate*

Latin verb *experior*—to know by experience. For Perkins, our experience of the covenant of grace begins with humiliation.[53] God "softens" our hearts by giving us a "sight of sin" arising from our knowledge of the law and a "sorrow for sin" arising from our knowledge of His displeasure.[54] Perkins equated this "pricking in the heart" with the "spirit of bondage" that the apostle Paul mentions in Romans 8:14. "This sorrow," says Perkins, "is called the *spirit of bondage to fear*; because when the Spirit has made a man see his sins, he sees further the curse of the law, and so he finds himself to be in bondage under Satan, hell, death, and damnation: at which most terrible sight his heart is smitten with fear and trembling."[55] Once this spirit of bondage takes hold, the result is "holy desperation."[56] Simply put, we recognize that we will never attain salvation by any strength or goodness of our own. Perceiving this, we acknowledge that

---

Plea for Preaching, ed. Don Kistler (Morgan, Pa.: Soli Deo Gloria, 2002), 94–128.

53. For more on this, see J. Stephen Yuille, "Ready to Receive: Humbling and Softening in William Perkins's Preparation of the Heart," *Puritan Reformed Journal* 5 (2013): 91–106.

54. William Perkins, *A Treatise Tending Unto a Declaration, whether a man be in the estate of damnation, or in the estate of grace*, in *The Works of William Perkins* (London, 1608), 1:363.

55. Perkins, *Tending Unto a Declaration*, 1:364. Perkins was careful to acknowledge that this experience of humiliation varies in degree and expression from person to person; that is to say, the issue is not the magnitude of our sorrow, but whether or not we are convinced that our righteousness is unacceptable in God's sight. "It is often seen in a festered sore," writes Perkins, "that the corruption is let out as well with the pricking of a small pin as with the wide lance of a razor." *Tending Unto a Declaration*, 1:364–65.

56. Perkins, *Tending Unto a Declaration*, 1:365.

we are without moral virtues adequate to commend ourselves to God, and that anything short of damnation is a mercy.

Having thereby softened our hearts, God now causes faith to "breed." For a better understanding of how God cultivates faith in the heart, Perkins appealed to the fact "that a sinner is often compared to a sick man in the Scriptures."[57] His point is that disease is to the body as sin is to the soul; moreover, the method of curing disease points to the method of curing sin.[58] When we are convinced we suffer from a disease, we immediately call for the doctor. When the doctor arrives, we yield ourselves to his counsel and willingly accept whatever remedy he prescribes. The same is true when it comes to faith in Christ. When we are absolutely convinced of our need, we submit to His cure. God leads us to "ponder most diligently" His great mercy offered in Christ, and He brings us to acknowledge our "need of Christ" whereby we pray, "O God, be merciful to me a sinner."[59]

Accompanying this faith is repentance, which Perkins defines as "a work of grace, arising of a godly sorrow; whereby a man turns from all his sins unto God, and brings forth fruits worthy amendment of life." For Perkins, God produces repentance by "steps and degrees." There must be: (1) the knowledge of the law of God, the nature of sin, the guilt of sin, and the judgment of God; (2) the application of this knowledge to the heart by the Spirit of bondage;

---

57. Perkins, *Tending Unto a Declaration*, 1:365.

58. Perkins, *Tending Unto a Declaration*, 1:365–66.

59. Perkins, *Tending Unto a Declaration*, 1:365.

(3) the consequent fear and sorrow; (4) the knowledge of the gospel; (5) the application of this knowledge to the heart by the Spirit of adoption; (6) the consequent joy and sorrow; and (7) the "turning of the mind, whereby a man determines and resolves with himself to sin no more as he hath done, but to live in newness of life."[60]

From humiliation, faith, and repentance, our experience of the covenant of grace moves to obedience. Perkins viewed the law as the point of contact between the covenant of works and the covenant of grace since obedience is fundamental to both covenants. He also asserted that the focus shifts between the two covenants from our obedience to Christ's obedience—the covenant of works having been fulfilled in the covenant of grace. For Perkins, therefore, we are free to obey the law in accordance with the new covenant. In his exposition of Matthew 7:21–23, he affirms that those who profess Christ's name seek to do the Father's will.[61] He defines the Father's will in terms of two texts in Scripture. The first is John 6:40, where Christ declares, "And this is the will of him that sent me, that every one which seeth the Son, and believeth on him, may have everlasting life: and I will raise him up at the last day." The second text is 1 Thessalonians 4:3–4, where the apostle Paul

---

60. William Perkins, *Two Treatises. I. Of the nature and practice of repentance. II. Of the combat of the flesh and spirit*, in *The Works of William Perkins* (London, 1608), 1:453.

61. For an analysis of Perkins's exposition of Christ's Sermon on the Mount, see J. Stephen Yuille, *Living Blessedly Forever: The Sermon on the Mount and the Puritan Piety of William Perkins* (Grand Rapids: Reformation Heritage Books, 2012).

writes, "For this is the will of God, even your sanctification, that ye should abstain from fornication: that every one of you should know how to possess his vessel in sanctification and honour." Based on these verses, Perkins maintains that "the doing of the Father's will" stands in three things: faith, repentance, and new obedience.[62]

Simply put, "new obedience" is the fruit of faith and repentance, whereby a man "endeavors himself to yield obedience to all God's commandments, from all the powers and parts both of his soul and his body." It is called *new*, because "it is a renewing of that in man whereto he was perfectly enabled by creation."[63] Perkins believed the affections are the inclination of the soul to a particular object. The soul loves whatever it perceives as good, and this love is manifested in desire (when the object is absent) and delight (when the object is present). Conversely, the soul hates whatever it perceives as evil, and this hatred is manifested in fear (when the object is absent) and sorrow (when the object is present). Prior to Adam's fall in the garden, man's love was set on God and, consequently, his affections were well directed. When Adam fell, however, the object of man's love changed. In his fallen condition, his love is no longer set on God but on self. In a state of regeneration, the Holy Spirit renews our love for God, and the result is new obedience. Perkins elaborates, "Sanctified

---

62. Perkins, *Christ's Sermon in the Mount*, 3:245. Perkins sees *faith* in John 6:40 and *repentance* (i.e., sanctification) and *new obedience* in 1 Thessalonians 4:3.

63. Perkins, *Christ's Sermon in the Mount*, 3:246.

affections are known by this, that they are moved and inclined to that which is good, to embrace it: and are not commonly affected and stirred with that which is evil, unless it be to eschew it."[64]

For Perkins, this experience of the covenant of grace in humiliation, faith, repentance, and obedience was absolutely essential. We must seek "the graces of God's children who are regenerate, even true faith, true repentance, and new obedience, and not rest in other gifts though they be most excellent."[65] He was convinced that many people err at this very point because they satisfy themselves with "a general persuasion of God's mercy."[66] But this "general persuasion" is not the same thing as genuine faith and repentance. It may produce "reformation of life," but it never produces "new obedience."

Expectedly, this discussion of "a general persuasion of God's mercy" leads to Perkins's handling of the doctrine of assurance. By the late sixteenth century, the issue of assurance loomed large within the Church of England because of the growing tendency on the part of many to take God's saving grace for granted. As Richard Lovelace explains, "The problem that confronts the Puritans as they look out on their decaying society and their lukewarm church is not simply to dislodge the faithful from the slough of mortal or venial sin, but radically to awaken those who are professing but not actual Christians, who are

---

64. Perkins, *Tending Unto a Declaration*, 1:371.
65. Perkins, *Christ's Sermon in the Mount*, 3:249.
66. Perkins, *Christ's Sermon in the Mount*, 3:247.

caught in a trap of carnal security."[67] The early Puritans in particular reacted to dead orthodoxy, which minimized the seriousness of sin and regarded mere assent to the truths of Scripture as sufficient for salvation. It thus became essential for them to distinguish between assurance and presumption. Perkins was particularly concerned with the prevalence of civility within the professing church. "If we look into the general state of our people," says he, "we shall see that religion is professed, but not obeyed; nay, obedience is counted as preciseness, and so reproached."[68] He was deeply concerned, therefore, about awakening a sleepy generation of church-goers from their false sense of security. As a result, he labored to lead his flock into a well-grounded assurance of salvation.[69]

To that end, Perkins produced several writings, in which he explains how we are to search our consciences for the least evidence of salvation based on Christ's saving work.[70] He viewed his efforts in this regard as part of a pastor's fundamental task in

---

67. Richard C. Lovelace, "The Anatomy of Puritan Piety: English Puritan Devotional Literature, 1600–1640," in *Christian Spirituality 3*, ed. L. Dupré and D. E. Saliers (New York: Crossroad, 1989), 303.

68. Perkins, *Christ's Sermon in the Mount*, 3:261.

69. Joel R. Beeke, *The Quest for Full Assurance: The Legacy of Calvin and His Successors* (Edinburgh: Banner of Truth Trust, 1999), 18.

70. For Perkins's treatment of the doctrine of assurance, see *A Treatise Tending unto a Declaration, whether a man be in the estate of damnation or in the restate of grace*; *A Case of Conscience, the greatest that ever was, how a man may know whether he be the child of God or no*; *A Discourse of Conscience, where is set down the nature, properties, and differences thereof, as also the way to get and keep a good conscience*; and *A Grain of Mustard-seed, or, the least measure of grace that is or can be effectual*

keeping "balance in the sanctuary" between divine sovereignty and human responsibility.[71] Pastors had to demonstrate how God's immovable will moved man's will and how to look for evidence of inclusion in God's covenant. They also had to instruct their people as to how to make their election sure.

According to Perkins, one of the principal means by which God imparts assurance is the covenant of grace. The golden chain of salvation (predestination, calling, justification, sanctification, and glorification) is linked to us through the preaching of God's gracious covenant. Perkins pointed to this covenant as a basis for assurance, maintaining that God becomes our God by means of the gracious covenant propounded in the gospel, promising pardon of sin in Christ. "What must we do to say truly and in assurance that God is our God?" Here are the basics of Perkins's answer:

> We must for our parts make a covenant with Him, unto which is required consent on either party; first on God's part, that He will be our God.... On our part is required consent.... When we receive the sacraments...there is required in our consent a further degree which stands in an outward consent of the heart, whereby a man takes God for his God; which is then begun, when first a man acknowledges and bewails his sins...when he endeavors to be reconciled to God...when he purposes never to sin

---

to salvation. These four treatises are found in *The Works of William Perkins* (London, 1608), vol. 1.

71. Irvonwy Morgan, *Puritan Spirituality* (London: Epworth, 1973), chap. 2.

> again. When this covenant is thus concluded by consent of both parties, a man may safely and truly say that God is his God. Now seeing we know these things, our duty is to labor to be settled and assured.... First in this assurance is the foundation of all true comfort: all the promises of God are hereupon grounded...and not only is it the foundation of all comfort in this life, but of all happiness after death itself...for by virtue of this covenant shall we rise again after death to life, glory, and immortality.[72]

Clearly, as far as Perkins was concerned, we are active in terms of our covenant relation with God. Yet he acknowledged that we never glean assurance from a conditional covenant alone, for human conditionality can never answer all the questions conjoined with human depravity and divine sovereignty. For Perkins, the covenant also contains an absolute relationship. Assurance does not flow from the covenant's conditional nature, which is connected to our performance, but from the covenant's absolute nature, which is grounded in God's gracious being and promises. Perkins comments, "God has spoken to us; He has made promise of blessing to us; He has made covenant with us; and He has sworn unto us. What can we more require of Him? What better ground of true comfort [is there]?" He adds, "The promise is not made to the work, but to the worker, and to the worker, not for the merit of

---

72. William Perkins, *A Godly and Learned Exposition Upon the Whole Epistle of Jude*, in *The Works of William Perkins* (London, 1631), 3:520.

his work, but for the merit of Christ."[73] Although Perkins encouraged people to strive after assurance, he ultimately pointed them to the one-sided grace of God, declaring that the covenant itself is a divine gift rooted in the merits of Christ. Assurance, in the final analysis, rests on God's faithfulness to His covenant promises, making even the fulfillment of the condition of faith on our part possible only by God's gracious gift.

For Perkins, faith is a supernatural gift by which we take hold of Christ with all the promises of salvation. The object of faith is Christ alone. Faith sees Christ, first, as the sacrifice on the cross for the remission of sins, then learns to experience Him as the strength to battle temptation, the comfort to endure affliction, and ultimately as everything needed in this life and the life to come. In sum, faith shows itself when "every several person does particularly apply unto himself, Christ with His merits, by an inward persuasion of the heart which comes none other way, but by the effectual certificate of the Holy Ghost concerning the mercy of God in Christ Jesus."[74]

Faith, therefore, has no meaning apart from Christ. "Faith is…a principal grace of God, whereby man is engrafted into Christ and thereby becomes one with Christ, and Christ one with him."[75] Perkins's numerous references to faith as an "instrument" or

---

73. William Perkins, *A Commentary or Exposition Upon the Five First Chapters of the Epistle to the Galatians*, in *The Works of William Perkins* (London, 1631), 2:243, 393.

74. Perkins, *Golden Chain*, 1:79–80.

75. Perkins, *Cases of Conscience*, 45.

Gisbertus Voetius (1589–1676)

Dutch theologian at the University of Utrecht known for combining academic theology and personal Christian devotion. Voetius referred to Perkins as "the Homer of practical Englishmen."

"hand" must be understood in this context. Faith is a gift of God's sovereign pleasure that moves us to respond to Christ through the preaching of the Word. Perkins's use of "instrument" or "hand" conveys the simultaneously passive and active role of faith in this redemptive activity. As Hideo Oki writes, "The connotation of 'instrument' suggests activity. This activity, however, is never simply 'positive'; on the contrary, it means that when it is most active, then it is moved and used by something other and higher than itself. Thus, in the midst of activity there is passivity, and in the midst of passivity it [is] most efficient in activity."[76] This is precisely what Perkins intended. Initially, faith is the passive "instrument" or "hand" granted by God to the sinner to receive Christ. Yet, precisely at the moment when Christ is received, faith responds to the gift of grace. Thus, the response is most active when it has completely yielded to the person it has received. This concept of faith, within the context of covenant, is the genius of Perkins's theology. His intense concern for the godly life arises alongside his equally intense concern to maintain the Reformation principle of salvation by grace alone, for we are never granted salvation on account of our faith but by means of faith.

Perkins's Legacy

Perkins was committed to proclaiming this experience of God's sovereign grace from humiliation to assurance and seeing it cultivated in others.

---

76. Hideo Oki, "Ethics in Seventeenth Century English Puritanism" (ThD diss., Union Theological Seminary, New York, 1960), 141.

Behind the industrious scholar, combative polemicist, exhaustive expositor, and prolific author, stood a pastor deeply concerned about the spiritual condition of the individual in the pew. For Perkins, there was a clear difference between speculative (notional) knowledge and sensible (inclinational) knowledge. The first involves the head alone, whereas the second involves the head and heart. With this distinction in view, he exhorts:

> We must labor for the power of this knowledge in ourselves, that we may know Christ to be our Savior, and may feel the power of His death to mortify sin in us, and the virtue of His resurrection to raise and build us up to newness of life for knowledge in the brain will not save the soul. Saving knowledge in religion is experimental, and he that is truly founded upon Christ feels the power and efficacy of His death and resurrection, effectually causing the death of sin, and the life of grace which both appear by new obedience.[77]

In Perkins's estimation, the Reformed theology of grace ("golden chain") was not a subject for mere academic debate and discussion, but it was crucial to the development of true Christian piety. Perkins was concerned that the church was full of people who possess a notional belief in God, yet remain worldly in their ultimate concerns and pursuits. He was convinced, therefore, that such people must experience an affective appropriation of God's sovereign grace,

---

77. Perkins, *Christ's Sermon in the Mount*, 3:259–60.

moving beyond intellectual assent to heartfelt dedication to Christ.

This emphasis is prevalent throughout Perkins's works. It is central, for example, in his sermons on the book of Jude. Jude reminds his readers that they "should earnestly contend for the faith which was once delivered unto the saints" (v. 3). Perkins declares that the faith "is nothing else but the wholesome doctrine of the gospel,"[78] consisting of two "general" heads: faith and love. He derives these two "heads" from 2 Timothy 1:13: "Hold fast the form of sound words, which thou hast heard of me, in faith and love which is in Christ Jesus." In short, "the wholesome doctrine of the gospel" contains things needful to be "believed" (faith) and things needful to be "practiced" (love). Accordingly, Perkins expounds twenty-one "grounds of doctrine to be believed"[79] and eleven "grounds of doctrine to be practiced,"[80] thereby demonstrating the relationship between faith and love.

In the following pages you will find these grounds with accompanying explanations drawn from across Perkins's works. It is hoped that these chapters will serve as a helpful introduction to his works and an insightful glimpse into his understanding of the wholesome doctrine of the gospel.

---

78. Perkins, *Works* (2014), 4:47.
79. Perkins, *Works* (2014), 4:47–72.
80. Perkins, *Works* (2014), 4:72–92.

SECTION ONE

Faith: Grounds of Doctrine to Be Believed

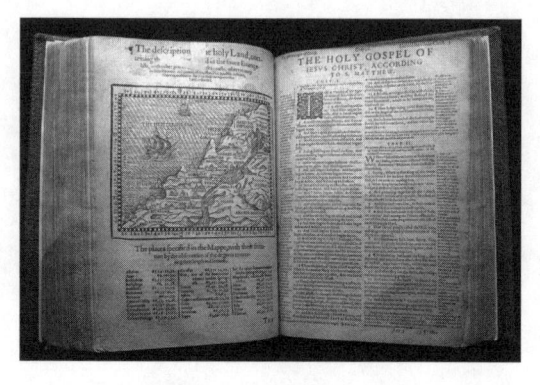

The Geneva Bible, 1560

An English Bible translation with marginal notes. Perkins used and often quoted this English translation in his works.

1

The Certainty of Scripture

All scripture is given by inspiration of God.
—2 Timothy 3:16

It is a thing most necessary that men should be assured that the doctrine of the gospel and the Scripture is not of man but of God.[1] This is the first thing which Paul stands upon in this epistle. It may be asked how this assurance is obtained. I answer, for the settling of our consciences that Scripture is the Word of God, there are two testimonies.

The first testimony is the evidence of God's Spirit, imprinted and expressed in the Scriptures. This is an excellency of the Word of God above all words and writings of men and angels. It contains thirteen points. The first is the purity of the law of Moses, whereas the laws of men have their imperfections. The second is that the Scriptures set down the true cause of all misery, namely sin, and the perfect remedy, namely the death of Christ. The third is the antiquity of Scripture, in that it sets down a history from the beginning of the world. The fourth is the prophecies of things in sundry books of Scripture,

---

1. *Commentary on Galatians*, ed. J. Stephen Yuille, vol. 2 of *The Works of William Perkins*, gen. ed. Joel R. Beeke and Derek W. H. Thomas (Grand Rapids: Reformation Heritage Books, 2015), 39–41.

which none could possibly foretell but God. The fifth is the confirmation of the doctrine of the prophets and apostles by miracles, that is, works done above and contrary to the strength of nature, which none can do but God. The sixth is the consent of all the Scriptures with themselves, whereas the writings of men often contradict one another. The seventh is the confession of enemies (namely heretics), who, when opposing Scripture, quote Scripture, and thereby confess to the truth thereof. The eighth is an unspeakable detestation that Satan and all wicked men bear to the doctrine of Scripture. The ninth is the protection and preservation of Scripture from the beginning to this hour by a special providence of God. The tenth is the constant profession of martyrs who have shed their blood for the gospel of Christ. The eleventh is the fearful punishments and judgments which have befallen those who have opposed the Word of God. The twelfth is the holiness of those who profess the gospel. The last is the effect and operation of the Word, for it is an instrument of God, in the right use whereof we receive the testimony of the Spirit of our adoption and are converted unto God.

The second testimony is from the prophets and apostles, extraordinary ambassadors of God, who represented His authority unto His church. They were the penmen of the Holy Spirit in setting down the true and proper Word of God. The apostles, above the rest, were eye-witnesses and ear-witnesses of the sayings and doings of Christ. Because they were guided by the infallible assistance of the Spirit in both preaching and writing, their testimony, touching the things which they wrote, must be authentic.

If it is said that counterfeit writings were published to the world under the name of the apostles, I answer that the apostles by their authority cut them off in their day. Therefore, Paul says, "If any man preach any other gospel…let him be accursed" (Gal. 1:9). The apostles provided that no counterfeits should arise under their names after their departure. For this reason, John, the last of the apostles, concludes the New Testament with this clause: "If any man shall add unto these things, God shall add unto him the plagues that are written in this book" (Rev. 22:18).

If anyone inquires as to the value of the church's testimony, I answer that, distinct from the apostles, its testimony is far inferior to the apostolic testimony concerning the Word of God. The church is to be ruled by the testimony of the apostles in the written Word, and the sentence of the church is not always certain nor joined with that evidence of the Spirit which accompanies every apostolic testimony.

Furthermore, if we are to receive these two testimonies, and benefit from them, we must yield subjection and obedience to the Word of God. In our obedience we will be assured that Scripture is indeed of God, as our Savior Christ says, "If any man will do his will, he shall know of the doctrine, whether it be of God, or whether I speak of myself" (John 7:17).

This doctrine touching the certainty of the Word is of great use. First, when the mind and conscience, by means of the double testimony mentioned above, plainly apprehend the certainty of the Word, a foundation is laid for the fear of God and justifying faith. Before we are assured that the Scripture is the Word of God, it is not possible that we should conceive and believe in the promises of God. The lack of this certainty, in many people, is an open door to heresy, apostasy, atheism, and all iniquity. Second, we see that the Church of Rome errs grossly in teaching that we cannot know the Scriptures to be the Word of God without the testimony of the church in these latter times, and that without it we could have no certainty of religion. The testimony of the Spirit, or the evidence thereof in Scripture, with the testimony of the apostles, will do the deed sufficiently, though the church should be silent.

2

The Sufficiency of Scripture

All scripture…is profitable for doctrine, for reproof, for correction, for instruction in righteousness: That the man of God may be perfect, thoroughly furnished unto all good works.
—2 Timothy 3:16–17

There are two kinds of application: mental and practical.[1] Mental application is concerned with the mind and involves either doctrine or reproof. When it involves doctrine, biblical teaching is used to inform the mind to enable it to come to a right judgment about what is to be believed. When it involves reproof, biblical teaching is used to recover the mind from error.

When false teaching is refuted during the exposition of Scripture, the following cautions should be observed. (1) Make sure that you thoroughly understand the issue involved or the state of the question to be discussed. (2) Reprove only the errors which currently trouble the church. Leave others alone if they lie dead in past history, or if they are not relevant to the people, unless you know that spiritual danger may still arise from them.… (3) If the error

---

1. *The Art of Prophesying*, Puritan Paperbacks (Edinburgh: Banner of Truth, 1996), 61–65.

is not foundational to the gospel, your refutation should be done not only in a truly Christian fashion (as should always be the case) but also in a friendly manner. Gentle and brotherly disagreement is called for here.

Practical application has to do with lifestyle and behavior, and it involves instruction and correction. Instruction is the application of doctrine to enable us to live well in the context of family, state, and church. It involves both encouragement and exhortation (Rom. 15:4). Correction is the application of doctrine in a way that transforms lives marked by ungodliness and unrighteousness. It involves admonition. Such admonition must be done generally at first, without reference to specific circumstances. This principle is well illustrated in 2 Samuel 12, where Nathan first made David aware of his sin by means of a general parable. Paul appears to have adopted a similar approach in Acts 19:26–37. If this kind of reproof does not bear fruit, it should be expressed in more detailed ways (1 Tim. 5:20). But our expression of hatred for sin must always be accompanied by an obvious love for the person who has sinned. Whenever possible, the minister should include himself in his reproofs. In this way his preaching, teaching, and counseling will be expressed in a mild and gentle spirit (Dan. 4:16–19; 1 Cor. 4:6; Gal. 2:15).

We can employ these different kinds of application (doctrine, reproof, instruction, and correction) with respect to every sentence of Scripture. It may

The Sufficiency of Scripture 9

be valuable to use the example of Matthew 10:28,[2] where Jesus urges the disciples not to fear those who can kill only the body, but rather to fear Him who can destroy both body and soul in hell....

Concerning doctrine: (1) It is necessary for us to confess publicly the doctrine we know whenever the need arises. (2) We must make this confession even if it means risking the loss of our possessions and lives. (3) We should despise the value of our lives in comparison to the value we place on Christ and His truth. (4) Eternal punishments (experienced in both soul and body) are prepared for those who are not afraid to deny Christ and His truth. (5) God is intent and ready to rule and guide us, to enable us to make our confession aright. (6) The providence of God is not only general but particular, and it includes the tiniest details, even the hairs of our head.

Concerning reproof: (1) It is a mistake to think it is adequate merely to embrace in the heart the faith and right views of religion. It is equally mistaken to imagine that it is within human power to grant or affirm anything before men...especially when life seems to be in imminent danger of ending. (2) Epicureans are in error when they deny divine providence, thinking it beneath the majesty of God to take care of human affairs. (3) Stoics are in error when they imagine that all things are governed by fate or by some irresistible and violent necessity. (4) Those who displace the wise ordination of divine

---

2. Perkins takes this example from the Lutheran Matthias Flacius Illyricus (1520–1575).

providence with chance and fortune are mistaken. (5) Pelagians are in error in attributing more than is warranted to man's strength, as though it were in men's power to embrace the faith at their own pleasure or to continue steadfastly in it and fearlessly confess it to the end. (6) Others err when they depend more on outward things and unstable riches than on the power and goodness of God.

Concerning instruction: (1) We must, to the full extent of our power, strive to have the true fear of God in view because we have now learned that the one God is to be feared above all men. (2) We must learn to despise human things to such an extent that we always desire to leave this world and be with Christ in heaven. (3) Consideration of God's special providence should teach us to think of the presence of God as all-seeing and all-knowing, to seek His help, and to believe that He helps in all things and that He is able and willing to deliver us from all danger when it is fitting.

Concerning correction: (1) These words of Christ correct the negligence of those who do not pray for sincere love, so that inflamed with it they would not refuse to lay down their life for His name. (2) There is here, too, a criticism of the negligence of those who do not acknowledge or see the providence of God showing itself in all things. (3) There is reproof here for those who do not give thanks to God for promising in His providence to govern and defend us in everything that concerns us. (4) Those who abuse God's good creation are rebuked, since it is clear He takes care of all things.

The Sufficiency of Scripture

We can handle any passage of Scripture in this way. But we should not try to expound every doctrine on every occasion, but only those which we can apply appropriately to the present experiences and condition of the church. We must choose carefully, lest those who hear God's Word expounded are overwhelmed by the sheer number of applications.

3

God's Holiness

But to us there is but one God, the Father, of whom are all things.
—1 Corinthians 8:6

Moses, desiring to see God's face, was permitted to see but His hinder parts (Ex. 33:20–23).[1] No one can describe God by His nature but by His effects and properties. God is an essence: spiritual, simple, infinite, most holy. I say, first, that God is an essence to show that He is a thing absolutely subsisting in Himself and by Himself, not receiving His being from any other. Herein He differs from all creatures, which have subsisting and being from Him alone.

God is a spiritual essence because He is not any kind of body. Neither has He the parts of the bodies of men or other creatures but is in nature an invisible spirit, not subject to man's senses.

God is a simple essence because His nature admits no manner of composition of matter or form

---

1. *An Exposition of the Symbol, or the Creed of the Apostles*, in *The Foundation of Christian Religion Gathered into Six Principles; An Exposition of the Symbol, or the Creed of the Apostles; An Exposition of the Lord's Prayer*, ed. Ryan Hurd, vol. 5 of *The Works of William Perkins*, gen. ed. Joel R. Beeke and Derek W. H. Thomas (Grand Rapids: Reformation Heritage Books, 2017), 19–20.

of parts. The creatures are compounded of various parts and natures, but there is no such thing in God, for whatever thing He is, He is the same by one and the same singular and indivisible essence.

God is an infinite essence, and that divers ways: (1) infinite in time because He is without beginning or end; and (2) infinite in place because He is everywhere and excluded nowhere, within all places and beyond all places.

God is a most holy essence—that is, of infinite wisdom, mercy, love, goodness, etc. He alone is rightly termed "most holy" because holiness is of His very nature, whereas among the most excellent creatures it is otherwise. The creature is one thing, and the creature's holiness is another thing.

Thus, we see what God is, and it is for this reason that He describes Himself as "Jehovah Elohim" (Ex. 3:6, 14). Paul describes Him as the king "eternal, immortal, invisible, the only wise," to whom is due "honour and glory for ever and ever" (1 Tim. 1:17).

There is not, neither can there be, any more gods than one. The Apostles' Creed states, "I believe in God," not "in gods." The Nicene Creed and the Athanasian Creed explain the words of the Apostles' Creed in this manner: "I believe in one God." In former times, some held erroneously that two gods were the beginning of all things—one of good things and the other of evil things. Others held that there was one God in the Old Testament and another in the New Testament. Others, namely the Valentinians, held that there were thirty couples of gods, and the heathen people (as Augustine reports) worshiped thirty thousand gods. Yet we, who are members of God's church, must hold to and believe in one God alone and no more. "Know therefore this day, and consider it in thine heart, that the LORD he is God in heaven above, and upon the earth beneath: there is none else" (Deut. 4:39). There is "one Lord, one faith, one baptism, one God and Father of all..." (Eph. 4:5–6).

Some say that Scripture mentions many gods: magistrates are called gods (Ps. 82:6), Moses is called Aaron's god (Ex. 4:16), and the devil and idols are called gods (2 Cor. 4:4). But they are not properly or by nature gods, for in that respect there is only one God. They are so termed in other respects. Magistrates are gods because they are vice-gerents placed in the room of the true God to govern their subjects. Moses is Aaron's god because he was in the room of God to reveal His will to Aaron. The devil is a god because the hearts of the wicked world give the honor unto him which is peculiar to the ever-living God. Idols are called gods because they are such in men's conceits and opinions, who esteem them as gods. Therefore, Paul says an idol is nothing in the world (1 Cor. 8:4)—that is, nothing in nature subsisting, or nothing in respect of the divinity ascribed to it.

To proceed forward, to believe in this one God is to know and acknowledge Him as He has revealed Himself in His Word, to believe Him to be our God, and to put all our trust in Him. To this purpose Christ says, "And this is life eternal, that they might know thee the only true God, and Jesus Christ, whom thou hast sent" (John 17:3). Now the knowledge here meant is not a bare or general knowledge, for that the devils have, but a more special knowledge whereby I know God not only to be God but also to be my God and thereupon do put my confidence in Him.

4

God's Excellency

I am the Almighty God.
—Genesis 17:1

The nature of God is His most lively and most perfect essence.[1] The perfection of the nature of God is the absolute constitution thereof, whereby it is wholly complete within itself (Ex. 3:13–14; Acts 17:24). The perfection of His nature is either its simpleness or its infiniteness.

The simpleness of God is that by which He is void of all logical relation in arguments. He has not in Him subject or adjunct (John 5:26; 14:6; 1 John 1:5–7). Hence it is manifest that to have life and to be life, to be in light and to be light, are all one in God. Neither is God subject to generality or speciality, whole or parts, matter or that which is made of matter. If He were, there would be divers things in God, and one more perfect than another. Therefore, whatever is in God is His essence, and all that He is, He is by essence. The saying of Augustine is fit to prove this: "In God, to be, and to be just or mighty, are all one. But in the mind of man, it is not all one to be, and to be mighty or just. For the mind may be destitute of these virtues, and yet a mind."

---

1. *Golden Chain*, in *Works* (1631), 1:11–13.

Hence it is manifest that the nature of God is immutable and spiritual. God's immutability is that by which He is void of all composition, division, and change (James 1:17). We read that God "repents" (Gen. 6:6), but the meaning is that God changes the action, as men do that repent. Therefore, repentance signifies not any mutation in God, but in His actions, and such things as are made and changed by Him. God's nature is spiritual, in that it is incorporeal, and therefore invisible (John 4:24; 2 Cor. 3:17; Col. 1:15; 1 Tim. 1:17).

The infiniteness of God is twofold: His eternity and exceeding greatness. God's eternity is that by which He is without beginning and ending (Ps. 90:2; Rev. 1:8). God's exceeding greatness is that by which His incomprehensible nature is everywhere present, both within and beyond the world (1 Kings 8:27; Ps. 145:3; Jer. 23:14). Hence it is plain, first, that He is only one, and that indivisible, not many (Deut. 4:35; 1 Cor. 8:4; Eph. 4:5), and there can be but one thing infinite in nature. Second, it is evident that God is the knower of the heart, for nothing is hidden from that nature which is within all things and beyond all things, which is included in nothing nor excluded from anything (1 Kings 8:39; Ps. 139:1–2).

To this point, we have spoken of the perfection of God's nature, now follows the life of God by which the divine nature is in perpetual action, living and moving in itself (Ps. 42:2; Heb. 3:12). The divine nature is especially in perpetual operation by three attributes which manifest the operation of God toward His creatures. These are His wisdom, will, and omnipotence.

The wisdom of God is that by which He does, not by certain notions abstracted from the things themselves, but by His own essence, not successively and by discourse of reason, but by one eternal and immutable act of understanding, distinctly and perfectly know Himself and all other things, though infinite, whether they have been or not (Ps. 147:5; Matt. 11:27; Heb. 4:13). God's wisdom has these parts: His foreknowledge and counsel. The foreknowledge of God is that by which He most assuredly foresees all things that are to come (Acts 2:23; Rom. 8:29). This is not properly spoken of God but by reason of men to whom things are past or to come. The counsel of God is that by which He does most rightly perceive the best reason of all things that are done (Prov. 8:14).

The will of God is that by which He most freely and justly, with one act, wills all things (Rom. 9:18; Eph. 1:5; James 4:15). God wills that which is good by approving it and that which is evil (in as much as it is evil) by disallowing and forsaking it. And yet He voluntarily permits evil because it is good that there should be evil (Ps. 81:12; Acts 14:16). The will of God, by reason of divers objects, has divers names and is called either love and hatred or grace and justice....

The omnipotence of God is that by which He is most able to perform every work (Matt. 19:26). Some things are excepted. First, such things as are contrary to His Word; God cannot lie (2 Tim. 2:1–3; Titus 1:2). Second, such things as are contrary to His nature; God cannot destroy Himself, nor can He not beget His Son from eternity. Third, such things as imply a contradiction; God cannot make truth false, or that which is, when it is not, to be.

God's power may be distinguished into an absolute and actual power. God's absolute power is that by which He can do more than He either does or will do (Matt. 3:9; Phil. 3:21). God's actual power is that by which He causes all things to be, which He freely wills (Ps. 135:6).

5

God Triune

For there are three that bear record in heaven, the Father, the Word, and the Holy Ghost: and these three are one.

—1 John 5:7

The three persons are those who, subsisting in one Godhead, are distinguished by incommunicable properties (Gen. 19:24; John 1:1).[1] They are, therefore, coequal and are distinguished not by degree but by order.

The constitution of a person is when a personal property, or the proper manner of subsisting, is adjoined to the deity (or the one divine nature). Distinction of persons is that by which, albeit every person is one and the same perfect God, the Father is not the Son or the Holy Spirit, but the Father alone; and the Son is not the Father or the Holy Spirit, but the Son alone; and the Holy Spirit is not the Father or the Son, but the Holy Spirit alone. Neither can they be divided by reason of the infinite greatness of that most simple essence, which one and the same, is wholly in the Father, wholly in the Son, and wholly in the Holy Spirit, so that in these there is diversity of persons but unity in essence.

---

1. *Golden Chain*, in *Works* (1631), 1:14–15.

The communion of the persons, or rather the union, is that by which each is in the rest and with the rest by reason of the unity of the Godhead. And, therefore, each one possesses, loves, and glorifies the others, and works the same thing (Prov. 8:22, 30; John 1:1; 5:19; 14:10).

There are three persons: the Father, the Son, and the Holy Spirit (Matt. 3:16–17). The Father is a person without beginning, from all eternity begetting the Son (Heb. 1:3; 2:7). In the generation of the Son, these properties must be noted. (1) He who begets and He who is begotten are together, and not one before another in time. (2) He who begets communicates with Him who is begotten, not one part but His whole essence. (3) The Father begot the Son, not out of Himself but within Himself. The incommunicable property of the Father is to be unbegotten, to be a Father, to beget. He is the beginning of actions because He begins every action of Himself, effecting it by the Son and the Holy Spirit (Rom. 11:36; 1 Cor. 8:6).

The other two persons have the Godhead, or the whole divine essence of the Father by communication, namely, the Son and the Holy Spirit. The Son is the second person, begotten of the Father from all eternity (John 1:14; Rom. 8:32; Col. 1:15; Heb. 1:5). Although the Son is begotten of His Father, yet He is of and by Himself very good. For He must be considered either according to His essence or according to His filiation or sonship. In regard of His essence, He is (that is, of and by Himself) very God (*autotheos*), for the deity which is common to all three persons is not begotten. But as He is a person, and the Son of the

Father, He is not of Himself but from another, for He is the eternal Son of the Father. Thus, He is truly said to be "very God of very God." For this cause, He is said to be sent from the Father (John 8:42). This sending takes not away the equality of essence and power, but declares the order of the persons (John 5:18; Phil. 2:6). He is the Word of the Father, not a vanishing but essential Word, because as a word is, as it were, begotten of the mind, so is the Son begotten of the Father....[2] The property of the Son is to be begotten. His proper manner of working is to execute actions from the Father by the Holy Spirit (1 Cor. 8:6).

The Holy Spirit is the third person, proceeding from the Father and the Son (John 15:26; 16:13–14; Rom. 8:9). Although the Father and the Son are two distinct persons, yet they are both one beginning of the Holy Spirit. What is the essential difference between proceeding and begetting neither Scripture determines nor the church knows. The incommunicable property of the Holy Spirit is to proceed. His proper manner of working is to finish an action, effecting it as from the Father and the Son.

---

2. Perkins appeals to Gregory of Nazianzus, *Oration of the Son*, and Basil of Caesarea, *Preface to John's Gospel*.

6

God's Sovereignty

Are not two sparrows sold for a farthing? and one of them shall not fall on the ground without your Father.
—Matthew 10:29

"For thine is the kingdom, and the power, and the glory, for ever. Amen" (Matt. 6:13).[1] These words contain the reason of the former six petitions. We must observe two things in general. First, they are not a reason to move God whose will is unchangeable, but to persuade the child of God who prays thus that God will grant his requests. Second, this reason is not peculiar to the last petition, but generally belongs to them all....

"Thine is the kingdom." This imports three things in God. First, He is all-sufficient of Himself to do all things, needing no help nor instrument beside His sovereign will. "I am the Almighty God" (Gen. 17:1). Second, He has a sovereign right and title to all things in heaven and earth, as a king has a right to those things which belong to his territories

---

1. *Sermon on the Mount*, *Digest or Harmony of the Books of the Old and New Testaments; Combat Between Christ and the Devil; Sermon on the Mount*, ed. J. Stephen Yuille, vol. 1 of *The Works of William Perkins*, gen. ed. Joel R. Beeke and Derek W. H. Thomas (Grand Rapids: Reformation Heritage Books, 2014), 1:493–97.

and jurisdiction. Third, He has sovereign rule and authority over all things in heaven and earth, governing them as He pleases and bringing them into absolute subjection.

Further, the kingdom of God is twofold. First, the kingdom of His providence is that whereby He rules and governs all things in heaven and earth, even the devil and all his angels and instruments. Second, the kingdom of grace is that whereby He governs His church by His Word and Spirit. Both these are here to be understood.

The kingdom is here called God's for two causes. First, to show that God has His kingdom of Himself and from Himself alone; thus, the kingdom of grace and of providence are both His. Second, to distinguish God from earthly kings, for though they have a kingdom, power, and glory, as Daniel tells Nebuchadnezzar (Dan. 4:22), yet they have all these from God, not of themselves. But God has them of Himself, and not from any other....

"Thine is the power." By "power" is meant an ability in God whereby He can do whatever He will and more than He will do. For the better conceiving of it, note these two things. First, God is not only powerful, but even power itself in regard of His nature as He is goodness and wisdom, etc. Men and angels are called powerful, as receiving power from God, but only God is power itself because His nature is infinite in power, as in all other properties. Second, power and will in God are one and the same. For our better conceiving of them, they may be distinguished, but in themselves they differ not, for God's willing of a thing is the effecting and doing of it. It is not so in us, for we will many things which we cannot do. But whatever God wills that He does; and that which He cannot do, He cannot will. The Scripture says that God cannot lie, or deny himself, or die (2 Tim. 2:13; Titus 1:2). As He cannot do these things, so neither can He will them. They are no works of power, but of weakness and frailty, and therefore is God omnipotent because He can neither do nor will the same.

Here also we say God's power is His own, that is, of Himself alone, not received from any other, as is also said of kingdom and glory, to distinguish the true God from all creatures who have not power, or kingdom, or glory of themselves, but from God, whereas all these are of Himself alone.

"Thine is the glory." By "glory" is meant excellence and majesty. This property rightly arises from the former two, for seeing He has an absolute sovereignty over all things and power answerable to dispose and govern them at His pleasure, therefore by right all glory, majesty, and excellence belong unto Him....

This reason, thus conceived and understood, has many uses. First, it contains a notable ground of trust and confidence in God, and of prayer to God in all distress of life and death. We have a Father to whom belongs the kingdom, power, and glory. His power assures us that He is able to help us....

Second, these words are a notable form of giving thanks and praise to God. When the heavenly creatures are said to give thanks to God, they do it to this effect: "Thou art worthy, O Lord, to receive glory and honour and power" (Rev. 4:11).... These three (kingdom, power, and glory) generally comprehend all matter of praise and thanksgiving unto God; yea, it is a sum of all the psalms of praise. When David blessed God, it was to this effect: "Thine, O LORD, is the greatness, and the power, and the glory, and the victory, and the majesty: for all that is in heaven and in the earth is thine: thine is the kingdom, O LORD, and thou art exalted as head above all. Both riches and honour come of thee, and thou reignest over all; and in thine hand is power and might..." (1 Chron. 29:11–12).

Third, here we see a way whereby we may obtain the things we ask of God; namely, we must confess our own unworthiness, taking shame and confusion to ourselves, and giving all praise and honor and glory to God. Thus did Jacob, "I am not worthy of the least of all the mercies, and of all the truth, which thou hast shewed unto thy servant" (Gen. 32:10).... Coming in humility of heart, renouncing ourselves and all that we can do, and endeavoring to give all glory to God, we shall find mercy with the Lord for the obtaining of all our requests.

Fourth, these words teach that God is to be feared above all creatures. Although Satan and earthly monarchs have dominion and power, yet it is not of themselves, but from God. They can do nothing but by the power and permission from God. But God of Himself can punish and destroy.

Fifth, hereby we must be moved to love God and to yield obedience unto Him in all good duties. He shows His sovereignty and power for all good things to us, so that we may give the glory of all to Him that gives them.

7

God's Mercy

Therefore hath he mercy on whom he will.
—Romans 9:18

Predestination is the counsel of God touching the last end or estate of man beyond this temporal or natural life.[1] In terms of natural life, we are all alike, and this kind of life is in the counsel of God only a preparation and step unto the spiritual and heavenly life. The supreme end of predestination is the manifestation of God's glory, partly in His mercy and partly in His justice....

The common means of accomplishing this counsel is twofold: the creation and the permission of the fall. The creation is that by which God made the whole man out of nothing according to His own image, yet changeable and endued with a natural life. The permission of the fall is that whereby God justly suffered Adam and his posterity to fall away, in that He did not hinder them when He was able, as being indeed bound to none to hinder. God is said not to hinder evil when He ceases after a sort from His operation, not illuminating the mind and not inclining the will to obey His voice. This permission of the evil of fault is by God's foreknowledge and

---

1. *A Treatise of Predestination*, in *Works* (1631), 1:606–11.

will, but only for the greater good of all, which would be hindered if God did not suffer evil. For if there were no sin, there would be no place for the patience of martyrs and for the sacrifice of Christ offered upon the cross, which infinitely exceeds all the sin of the whole world.... That which I have said of the permission of the fall, I also say of the fall permitted, saving that the permission is a means of the decree by itself, but the fall is a means (of accomplishing the decree) only by the ordination of God, who draws good out of evil....

Predestination has two parts: the decree of election and the decree of reprobation.... The decree of election is that whereby God has ordained certain men to His glorious grace, in the obtaining of their salvation and heavenly life by Christ. In the decree of election according to God's determination, there is (as we conceive) a double act. The former concerns the end, the latter concerns the means tending to the end....

The first act is a purpose, or rather a part and beginning of the divine purpose whereby God takes certain men who are to be created, unto His everlasting love and favor, passing by the rest, and makes them vessels of mercy and honor. This act is the sole will of God, without any respect of good or evil in the creature. God wrongs no one, although He chooses not all, because He is tied to no one, and because He has absolute sovereignty and authority over all creatures. We, who are men, give leave unto men, especially unto our friends, to do at their pleasure in many things as they themselves desire and to use their own discretions. The rich man is kind to

God's Mercy

whichever poor person he pleases, and he adopts one beggar and does not adopt another, and that without offering any injury. Now that liberty, which we yield unto man, must much more be granted unto God.

The second act in election is the purpose of saving or conferring glory whereby God ordains or sets apart the very same men, which were fallen in Adam, unto salvation and celestial glory. This act is in no wise to be severed from the former, but to be distinguished in the mind (for order's sake, and for the better unfolding of it), for as by the former men were ordained unto grace, so by this latter the means are subordinated whereby grace may be conferred and manifested. Therefore, the latter makes a way for the execution and accomplishing of the former. Moreover, this act has no inward impulsive cause over the good and beside the good pleasure of God. It is with regard to Christ the Mediator, in whom all are elected to grace and salvation. To dream of any election outside of Him is against all sense because He is the foundation of election to be executed in regard of the beginning, the means, and the end. Lastly, this act is not of men to be created, as was the former, but of men fallen away. Therefore, in this act, God respects the corrupted mass of mankind....

The decree of reprobation is a work of God's providence whereby He has decreed to pass by certain men, in regard of supernatural grace, for the manifestation of His justice and wrath in their due destruction. Or, it is His will whereby He suffers some men to fall into sin and inflicts the punishment of condemnation for sin. It has in like manner two acts.

The first is the purpose to forsake some men and to make known His justice in them. This act has a final cause but no impulsive cause outside of God, for it arises from God's mere good pleasure, with no respect of good or evil in the creature. The will of God is the cause of causes. Therefore, we must make our stand in it, and out of or beyond it no reason must be sought; yea, indeed, there is nothing beyond it. Moreover, every man is unto God as a lump of clay in the potter's hand (Rom. 9:21). Therefore, God, according to His supreme authority, makes vessels of wrath; He does not find them made. But He would not make them but find them made, if we were to say that He willed in His eternal counsel to pass by men only as they are sinners and not as they are men, for a cause most just though unknown to us. If God were to reject men because He foresaw that they would reject Him, reprobation would not depend upon God but upon men. And this is all one as if a man should say that God foresaw that some would choose Him and others refuse Him....

The second act is the ordaining of them to punishment or due destruction. This ordination...is either simple or comparative. The simple ordination is that whereby this man (suppose Peter or John) is ordained to punishment, and this ordination is of the most just will of God yet not without respect to original and actual sins. As men are actually damned for sin, so God has decreed to damn them for the same sin. Yet sin is not the cause of the decree of reprobation, but in regard of order it goes before in God's foreknowledge....

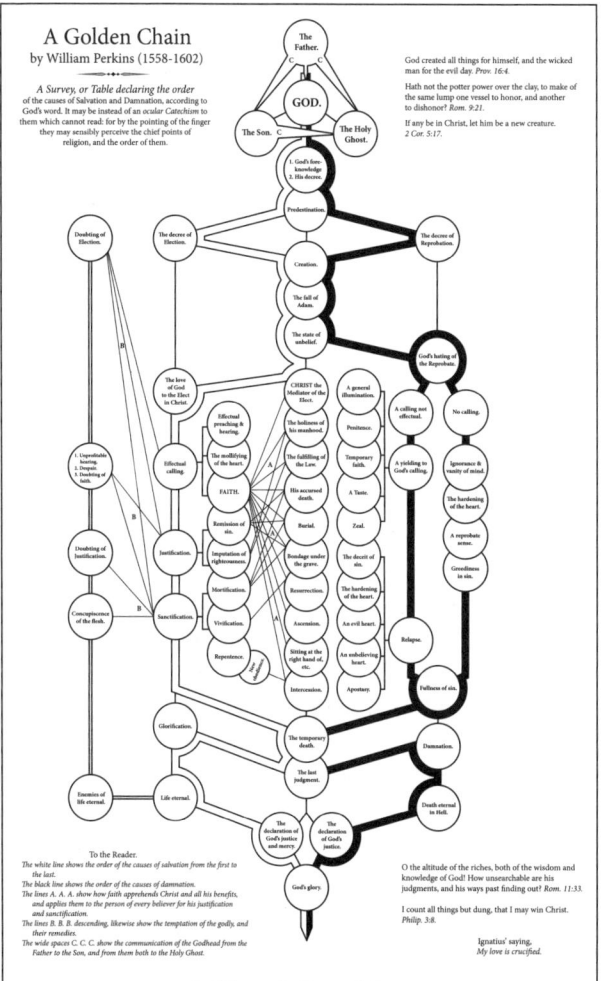

A Golden Chain
by William Perkins (1558-1602)

A Survey, or Table declaring the order of the causes of Salvation and Damnation, according to God's word. It may be instead of an *ocular Catechism* to them which cannot read: for by the pointing of the finger they may sensibly perceive the chief points of religion, and the order of them.

God created all things for himself, and the wicked man for the evil day. *Prov. 16:4.*

Hath not the potter power over the clay, to make of the same lump one vessel to honor, and another to dishonor? *Rom. 9:21.*

If any be in Christ, let him be a new creature. *2 Cor. 5:17.*

The Father.

GOD.

The Son. **The Holy Ghost.**

1. God's fore-knowledge
2. His decree.

Predestination.

Doubting of Election. — The decree of Election. — The decree of Reprobation.

Creation.

The fall of Adam.

The state of unbelief.

God's hating of the Reprobate.

The love of God to the Elect in Christ.

CHRIST the Mediator of the Elect. — A general illumination.

Effectual preaching & hearing. — The holiness of his manhood. — Penitence. — A calling not effectual. — No calling.

1. Unprofitable hearing.
2. Despair.
3. Doubting of faith.

Effectual calling. — The mollifying of the heart. — The fulfilling of the Law. — Temporary faith. — A yielding to God's calling. — Ignorance & vanity of mind.

FAITH. — His accursed death. — A Taste. — The hardening of the heart.

Doubting of Justification. — Remission of sin. — Burial. — Zeal. — A reprobate sense.

Justification. — Imputation of righteousness. — Bondage under the grave. — The deceit of sin. — Greediness in sin.

Concupiscence of the flesh. — Sanctification. — Mortification. — Resurrection. — The hardening of the heart.

Vivification. — Ascension. — An evil heart. — Relapse.

Repentance. — Sitting at the right hand of, etc. — An unbelieving heart.

Intercession. — Apostasy. — Fullness of sin.

Glorification. — The temporary death. — Damnation.

The last judgment.

Enemies of life eternal. — Life eternal. — The declaration of God's justice and mercy. — The declaration of God's justice. — Death eternal in Hell.

God's glory.

To the Reader.
The white line shows the order of the causes of salvation from the first to the last.
The black line shows the order of the causes of damnation.
The lines A. A. A. show how faith apprehends Christ and all his benefits, and applies them to the person of every believer for his justification and sanctification.
The lines B. B. B. descending, likewise show the temptation of the godly, and their remedies.
The wide spaces C. C. C. show the communication of the Godhead from the Father to the Son, and from them both to the Holy Ghost.

O the altitude of the riches, both of the wisdom and knowledge of God! How unsearchable are his judgments, and his ways past finding out? *Rom. 11:33.*

I count all things but dung, that I may win Christ. *Philip. 3:8.*

Ignatius' saying,
My love is crucified.

A Visual Catechism

Perkins published this chart in *A Golden Chain* to serve as "a Survey, or Table declaring the Order & Causes of Salvation & Damnation according to God's Word."

The ordination which stands in comparison is that whereby one man and not another, and this man rather than that, being in the like condition, is ordained to punishment. This serves to show the liberty of God's will in the dispensation of supernatural benefits. That God chooses this man and not that one declares the liberty and very great perfection of God. And, therefore, under the name of a householder, He challenges the same unto Himself when He says, "Is it not lawful for me to do what I will with mine own?" (Matt. 20:15). Although God destroys and condemns all those whom He forsakes, yet He is not unjust. For we ourselves in the daily killing and slaughtering of beasts will not be counted unjust, neither indeed are we. And yet, in comparison of God, we are not so much worth as a fly is in respect of us. If it is lawful for you to receive in or thrust out anyone from your house because you will, it were a point of desperate boldness to take the same right from God in His house. The cause of this comparative ordination is the sole will of God, yea, even without respect of any sin at all.

8

The Supremacy of Christ

I am Alpha and Omega, the beginning and the ending, saith the Lord, which is, and which was, and which is to come, the Almighty.

—Revelation 1:8

Christ is the beginning and the end. John expresses this by a comparison taken from the Greek alphabet.[1] "A" in the ABC of the Grecians is *alpha*. It is the first letter and, therefore, the beginning of all the letters. Omega is the last letter and, therefore, the end of all the letters. So, Christ says, "I am the beginning of all things and the end of all things." The first part of this similitude is found in these words: "I am Alpha and Omega"—that is, "I am as Alpha and Omega." The second part is found in these words: "the beginning and the end."…

"I am the beginning." Christ is said to be the beginning for two causes. First, He was the very first of all things; there was nothing before Him. He had a being when all creatures were not. Then He was the same as He is now. "In the beginning was the Word"—that is, the Son of God (John 1:1). He had

---

1. *Exposition of Revelation 1–3*, in *Exposition of Jude; Exposition of Rev. 1–3*, ed. J. Stephen Yuille, vol. 4 of *The Works of William Perkins*, gen. ed. Joel R. Beeke and Derek W. H. Thomas (Grand Rapids: Reformation Heritage Books, 2017), 4:357–58.

His being and subsisting when all other creatures wanted it and began to be. This proves the eternity of Christ, because He had His being before any creature. He was a substance and essence begotten of the Father before all worlds, not created as other creatures are or made of any other. Second, He is called the beginning because He gives a beginning to all creatures. All things were created by Him and had their being from Him. The apostle Paul says, "All things were created by him, and for him" (Col. 1:16). Hence we learn that when we go about any business in word or deed, we must begin it with invocation in the name of Christ, for He gives the beginning and proceeding to all things, and without His help we cannot have good success in anything.

"I am the ending." The same Christ is the end of all things, and that for two causes. First, He is the last of all things, and after Him is nothing subsisting and being; for all creatures, if they were left to themselves, would come to nothing. Whereas some creatures are eternal, it is not of themselves but by Him and from Him which is the end. But though they all should come to nothing, yet Christ would remain the same as He was forever—namely, the eternal Son and Word of the Father. This then should make us with full purpose of heart to cleave unto Christ in all things, if we would enjoy eternal happiness. For without Him is nothing but changing; and unless we have our stableness from Him, we cannot but come to an end. Second, He is the end because all things in heaven and earth were made to serve Him. All things were created "for him" (Col. 1:16)—that is, to serve for His glory and praise.

9

The Creation of Man

God created man in his own image.
—Genesis 1:27

Man was created and framed by the hand of God and made after the image of God.[1] Moses records the Lord speaking thus, "Let us make man in our image" (Gen. 1:26).... The image of God is nothing else but a conformity of man unto God whereby man is holy as God is holy. Paul says, "Put on the new man, which after God [that is, in God's image] is created in righteousness and true holiness" (Eph. 4:24). Now I reason thus: wherein the renewing of the image of God in man does stand, therein was it at the first. But the renewing of God's image in man does stand in righteousness and holiness; therefore, God's image wherein man was created at the beginning was a conformity to God in righteousness and holiness. Now whether God's image further consists in the substance of man's body and soul or in the faculties of both, Scripture speaks not.

This image of God has two principal parts: wisdom and holiness. Concerning wisdom, Paul says, "And have put on the new man, which is renewed in knowledge after the image of him that created him"

---

1. *Exposition of the Symbol*, 65–66.

(Col. 3:10). This wisdom consists in three points. (1) Adam knew God, his Creator, perfectly, for in his innocence he knew God so far forth as it was convenient for a creature to know his Creator. (2) Adam knew God's will so far forth as it was convenient for him to show his obedience thereunto. (3) Adam knew the wisdom and will of his Creator touching the creatures; for after he was created, the Lord brought every creature unto him, presenting them unto him as being lord and king over them, that he might give names unto them. From this it appears that Adam in his innocence knew the nature of all creatures and the wisdom of God in creating them, or else he could not have given them fit names. And when God brought Eve to Adam, he knew her at the first and said, "This is now bone of my bones, and flesh of my flesh: she shall be called Woman, because she was taken out of Man" (Gen. 2:23).

The second part of God's image in man is holiness and righteousness, which is nothing else but a conformity of the will and affections and of the whole disposition of man in both body and soul to the will of God, his Creator. Yet we must remember that Adam in his innocence had a changeable will so as he could will either good or evil. He was created with such liberty of will as that he could indifferently will either. And we must not think that the will of the creature was made unchangeably good, for that is peculiar to the will of God, and hereby is the Creator distinguished from the creature.

Here two things offer themselves to be considered. The first is why the man, and not the woman, is called "the image of God." He is so called not because holiness and righteousness are peculiar to him, which is common to both, but because God has placed more outward excellency and dignity in the person of a man than of a woman (1 Cor. 11:7). The second is how Christ should be called the image of God. He is so called for two special causes. First, He is of the same substance with the Father and, therefore, is His most absolute image (Col. 1:15) and, as the author of Hebrews says, He is "the brightness of his glory, and the express image of his person" (1:3). Second, God, being invisible, manifests Himself in Christ, in whom as in a glass we may behold the wisdom, goodness, justice, and mercy of God.

10

The Fall of Man

Wherefore, as by one man sin entered into the world, and death by sin; and so death passed upon all men, for that all have sinned.
—Romans 5:12

There are three things in original sin: (1) the punishment, which is the first and second death; (2) the guilt, which is the binding up of the creature unto punishment; and (3) the fault (or, the offending of God, under which I comprehend our guilt in Adam's first offense as also the corruption of the heart), which is a natural inclination and proneness to anything that is evil or against the law of God.[1] We say that the first (the punishment) is taken away after baptism in the regenerate. "There is therefore now no condemnation to them which are in Christ Jesus" (Rom. 8:1). We further say that the second (the guilt) is also taken away in those who are born anew. Considering there is no condemnation to them, there is nothing to bind them to punishment. Yet this caveat must be remembered, namely, that the guilt is removed from the regenerate person, not from the sin in the person. But more of this afterward. We say, thirdly, that the guilt in Adam's first offense is pardoned. Touching

---
1. *A Reformed Catholic*, in *Works* (1631), 1:561–62.

the corruption of the heart, I avouch two things. (1) The very power or strength whereby it reigns in man is taken away in the regenerate. (2) This corruption is abolished (as also the fault of every actual past sin) so far forth as it is the fault and sin of the man in whom it is. Indeed, it remains until death, and it is sin considered in itself so long as it remains, but it is not imputed unto the person. And in that respect it is as though it were not, it being pardoned.

Thus far we consent with the Church of Rome. Now the difference between us stands not in the abolishment but in the manner and measure of the abolishment of this sin. The papists teach that original sin is so far forth taken away after baptism that it ceases to be a sin properly and is nothing else but a want, defect, and weakness, making the heart fit and ready to conceive sin. They compare it to tinder, which, though it is no fire of itself, is very apt and fit to conceive fire. They deny it to be sin properly that they might uphold some of their gross opinions, namely, that a man in this life may fulfill the law of God and do good works void of sin, and that by them he may stand righteous at the bar of God's judgment.

But we teach otherwise. Although original sin is taken away in the regenerate, and that in sundry respects, it remains in them after baptism, not only as a want and weakness, but as a sin, and that properly—as may by these reasons be proved. First, Paul says, "Now then it is no more I that do it, but sin that dwelleth in me" (Rom. 7:17)—that is, original sin. The papists say that it is so called improperly, because it comes of sin and is an occasion of sin to be done. But, according to the circumstances of the text,

Joseph Hall (1574–1656)

An English delegate to the Synod of Dort (1618–1619) who also served as a bishop within the Church of England. On Perkins, Hall remarked, "He excelled in a distinct judgment, a rare dexterity in clearing the obscure subtleties of the schools, and in an easy explication of the most perplexed subjects."

it is sin properly, for in the following words Paul says that this sin, dwelling in him, made him to do the evil which he hated. And he cries out, "O wretched man that I am! who shall deliver me from the body of this death?" (Rom. 7:24). Hence, I reason thus: that which once was sin properly, and remaining in man makes him sin, and entangles him in the punishment of sin, and makes him miserable, is sin properly. But original sin does all these.

Second, some baptized and regenerate infants die the bodily death before they come to the years of discretion; therefore, original sin in them is sin properly. If it were not, they would not die, having no cause of death in them, "for the wages of sin is death" (Rom. 6:23) and death entered into the world "by sin" (Rom. 5:12). As for actual sin, they have none, if they die presently after they are born, before they come to any use either of reason or affection.

Third, that which lusts against the Spirit, and by lusting tempts, and in tempting entices and draws the heart to sin, is for nature sin itself. But concupiscence in the regenerate wars against the Spirit and tempts (Gal. 5:17). "God cannot be tempted with evil, neither tempteth he any man: But every man is tempted, when he is drawn away of his own lust, and enticed. Then when lust hath conceived, it bringeth forth sin" (James 1:13–15). And, therefore, it is sin properly, for such as the fruit is such is the tree. Augustine says, "Concupiscence, against which the spirit lusts, is sin because in it there is disobedience against the rule of the mind. And it is the punishment of sin because it befalls man for the merits of his disobedience, and it is the cause of sin."

11

Law and Gospel

The man which doeth those things shall live by them.
—Romans 10:5

The law and gospel are two parts of the Word of God.... By the law I understand that part of God's Word which promises life to those who obey.[1] By the gospel I understand that part which promises life to the believer.... The law and gospel consent (1) in their author, which is God; (2) in their general matter, for both require justice and righteousness to salvation; and (3) in their end, namely the glory of God. But the law and the gospel dissent in the following.

First, the moral law is written in nature by creation, yea, and since the fall we have some remainder of it in us: the Gentiles "shew the work of the law written in their hearts" (Rom. 2:15). But the gospel is not in nature but above the reach of created nature, much more corrupted nature. The ground of the law is the image of God, but the ground of the gospel is Jesus Christ.

---

1. *Exposition of Jude*, in *Exposition of Jude; Exposition of Rev. 1–3*, ed. J. Stephen Yuille, vol. 4 of *The Works of William Perkins*, gen. ed. Joel R. Beeke and Derek W. H. Thomas (Grand Rapids: Reformation Heritage Books, 2017), 53–54.

Second, the law will have us do something that we may be saved by it, and that is to fulfill it. The gospel requires no doing by us but only believing in Christ. Some object that believing is a work to be done. But the gospel requires it not as a work, but as it is an instrument and the hand of the soul to lay hold upon Christ (Rom. 3:21; 4:5; 10:5). Hence it is that the law requires righteousness inherent, but the gospel, righteousness imputed.

Third, the law is propounded to the unrepentant sinner to bring him to faith, but the gospel, to the believer to the begetting and increase of faith.

Fourth, the law shows sin, accuses, and reveals justice without mercy, but the gospel covers sin and is a qualification of the rigor of the law. The law says, "Cursed be he that confirmeth not all the words of this law to do them" (Deut. 27:26). The gospel qualifies this and says, "Except ye repent, ye shall all likewise perish" (Luke 13:3). Thus the law, which only manifests justice, is moderated by the gospel, which mingles mercy and justice together, justice upon Christ, mercy unto us.

Fifth, the law tells us what good works must be done; the gospel, how they must be done. The former declares the matter of our obedience; the latter directs us in the manner of obeying. The former is pleased with nothing but the deed; the latter signifies that God is pleased to accept the will and unfeigned endeavor for the deed itself.

Sixth, the law is no worker of grace and salvation, no, not instrumentally, for it is the ministry of death. The gospel alone works grace, though the law may be a hammer to break the heart and prepare the way to faith and repentance.

The papists hold that the law and gospel are one doctrine, differing only in that the law is darker and the gospel is plainer, the former is harder to fulfill and the latter is easier, the former is as the root of a tree and the latter is as the body and branches. By these premises they conclude that Christ is no Savior but an instrument for us to save ourselves through His giving us grace to keep the law; for a sinner must be saved by works if there is no difference between the law and the gospel, and if the law, which requires works, is not moderated by the gospel, which requires not works but faith.

12

The Incarnation

And the Word was made flesh.
—John 1:14

"Every spirit that confesseth not that Jesus Christ is come in the flesh is not of God" (1 John 4:3)—that is, every doctrine that denies that Christ has come in the flesh is not of God but of antichrist.[1] By "Word," I understand the eternal Son of God, the second person of the Trinity, the very substantial Word of the Father. It is added, "was made," not as though the Son of God was turned into flesh and ceased to be God's Son, but that "he took not on him the nature of angels; but he took on him the seed of Abraham" (Heb. 2:16). The meaning then is that the Son of God, abiding still the Word, took—that is, received into His person—our nature. He "took upon him the form of a servant" (Phil. 2:7).

The word "flesh" signifies, first, man's nature which Christ took to Himself, namely, a true nature of man, not phantastical or apparent only. Second, it signifies the whole nature of man consisting of true and perfect soul and body, with all things that belong to the entire nature of man, for if He had taken man's nature only in part, He had redeemed it but in

---

1. *Exposition of Jude*, 54–56.

part. Third, it signifies the properties of man in soul (mind, will, and affections) and in body (breadth, length, and circumscription). Fourth, it signifies the infirmities and frailties of man's nature without sin; where it must be noted that Christ took not all the infirmities of man's nature, such as sin and corruption, neither every personal infirmity of every person, such as blindness, gout, or every disease....

Now the sum of the whole ground is that the Son of God, the second person and so abiding, took unto Him the perfect nature of man, in all things being like unto us, sin only excepted. For the further clearing of this, consider these four conclusions.

First, the Son of God made man is not two distinct persons but one alone. How can this be? For as He is the Son of God He is a person, and as He is a man He is a person, as every man is, and therefore He is two persons. I answer, every man is a person because he subsists of himself, but the manhood of Christ subsists not in itself but in the second person only, so that Christ, God and man, is but one person. For even as body and soul make one man, so Godhead and manhood make but one Christ.

Second, this one person consists of two distinct natures, the Godhead and the manhood standing of body and soul.

Third, these two natures are united and joined into one person, for the Godhead takes the manhood and supports it.

Fourth, these two natures after conjunction remain distinct. The Godhead is not the manhood, neither on the contrary, but still distinguished: first, in regard of themselves; second, in regard of their properties, for the properties of the one are not the properties of the other; and, third, in regard of their actions, for the actions of the Godhead are not communicated to the manhood, neither is the work of one nature the work of the other.

The enemies of this doctrine are Jews who deny Christ is come in the flesh. They also include Jewish Arians, compounded heretics, who have withstood Christ's incarnation.... The papists are also enemies, for the substance of their doctrine robs Christ of His human nature, though they confess Him to be incarnate. They teach that since His death His body has been invisible and present in innumerable places at once. And so, they abolish the manhood of Christ, and turn it into the Godhead, seeing it has become infinite and uncircumscribed.

They allege that God can make Christ's body to be in many places at once. But we may not dispute what God can do, but what He will do, so far as He has revealed. It stands not with the power of God to do some things, as those which employ contradictions to be true at the same time. Of which nature this is—to make a true body to be in many places at once, yea, to be in heaven and everywhere on earth.

They further allege that His body is glorified and, therefore, may be in many places at once. But the words "this is my body" (Luke 22:19) were spoken before His glorification. Glorification takes away the corruption, but not the true properties of His body, as length, breadth, thickness, and circumscription.

They say that things joined together must be in the same place and cannot be severed, and therefore His manhood being joined to His Godhead, must be everywhere. But the antecedent is false, for things joined together may be the one in one place, the other in another, as the body of the sun is joined with its beams and light, and yet the body of the sun is in heaven, but the beams and light in the earth also.

13

Christ the Mediator

> *Who is a liar but he that denieth that Jesus is the Christ? He is antichrist, that denieth the Father and the Son.*
> —1 John 2:22

From this verse we may gather two things: (1) Jesus is Christ; and (2) it is a ground sustaining our whole salvation, for whosoever denies it is antichrist.[1] By *Christ*, I understand the anointed Savior and Redeemer, who is a King, Priest, and Prophet.

First, as He is a King, His power manifests itself in three things: (1) in saving and destroying not only the body, as other kings, but the soul; (2) in pardoning sins or retaining them; and (3) in making laws to bind consciences.

Second, His priestly office stands in two things: (1) in a power to offer a propitiatory sacrifice for the sins of all mankind; and (2) in making intercession to God for mankind.

Third, His prophetic office consists in three things: (1) in revealing to man the will of His Father; (2) in enlightening the mind to understand His Father's revealed will; and (3) in framing the heart to

---

1. *Exposition of Jude*, 56–58.

perform obedience unto it, together with the settling of it in the truth.

Thus, He is the Christ, that is, the anointed of God. But we must go further and understand by "Christ" a perfect Christ, a perfect Redeemer, without any partner, fellow, or deputy. If He has a partner, He is but half a redeemer, and if He has a fellow or deputy, how is He omnipotent or omnipresent? This is plain by testimony of Scripture. There is "none other name" (Acts 4:12); therefore, there is no fellow or partner. There is "one mediator," that is, but one (1 Tim. 2:5). "By himself [he] purged our sins" (Heb. 1:3), that is, without fellow or deputy. His priesthood is such as cannot pass from Him to another (Heb. 7:24)....

The chief adversary of this doctrine is the Roman Church which robs Christ of all three offices. First, they give part of His kingly office to the pope by allowing him to remit sins properly, to make laws to bind consciences properly, as God's laws do, which is a power equal to Christ's, and so they make him equal with Christ. Second, they give His priestly office to the Mass priests, who by their doctrine have power to offer a propitiatory sacrifice for the sins of the quick and dead; yea, every papist has a piece of it, because every one of them may satisfy the justice of God for his sins by his own merit. And for His intercession, the second work of His priesthood, that is dealt among the saints (among whom the virgin Mary has the greatest part) who are invocated as intercessors, not only by their prayers but by their merits in heaven. Third, they bestow His prophetic office upon every pope, who is without Scripture to determine infallibly, by an inward assistance of the Spirit locked up in his breast, of all matters concerning faith and manners, which is the proper office of Him who is the proper Doctor of His church....

The Roman Church denies Jesus to be Christ. It has not the Son, because it overturns His person and erases all His offices. Neither have they the Father, but an idol-god, and so consequently their doctrine is anti-Christian and heretical. For which cause the Reformed churches have justly separated from them, and so long as they deny this ground ought ever so to do.

14

Faith

For God so loved the world, that he gave his only begotten Son, that whosoever believeth in him should not perish, but have everlasting life.

—John 3:16

This faith consists of two things: knowledge and application of the thing known.[1] The knowledge is of Christ and His benefits, of which there must be some measure or else there can be no faith. "By his knowledge shall my righteous servant justify many" (Isa. 53:11). "And this is life eternal, that they might know thee the only true God, and Jesus Christ, whom thou hast sent" (John 17:3). This stands with reason, that the thing to be believed must first be known, for faith without knowledge is fancy.... The second thing in faith (which is the more principal) is an application of the things known; namely, of Christ and His benefits to ourselves. Herein stands the very substance of true faith, which is not caused by any natural affection of heart or action of will, but by the supernatural action of the mind enlightened by the Spirit of God, convincing us that Christ and His merits belong to us. That this personal application is required in true faith is proved by the following reasons.

---

1. *Exposition of Jude*, 59–61.

First, that which we lawfully ask in prayer we must believe by a special faith. In prayer we lawfully ask for the pardon of our sins and life everlasting by Christ; therefore, we must believe the pardon of our sins and life everlasting by Christ.... "What things soever ye desire, when ye pray, believe that ye receive them, and ye shall have them" (Mark 11:24). In every petition of prayer, our Savior requires two things: (1) a desire of things promised; and (2) a particular faith of things desired, standing in assurance that they shall be granted.

Second, whatever the Holy Spirit infallibly testifies to us particularly, we must believe it particularly. But the Holy Spirit particularly testifies by infallible testimony to every believer's conscience his own adoption and pardon of sin and acceptance to life everlasting, and therefore it must be particularly believed. Here the papists object, saying that this testimony of the Spirit of God is not certain but only probable, and that a man may be deceived in it. But the apostle Paul answers this objection: "the Spirit itself beareth witness with our spirit, that we are the children of God" (Rom. 8:16). He clears this testimony of fearfulness and weakness in the former words, where he says it is "not the spirit of fear" which we have received, but such a Spirit as makes us cry, "Abba, Father" with a strong voice. For further assuring us in this testimony, it is called the "seal" and "earnest" of the Spirit in our hearts (2 Cor. 1:22). There are no more sure and certain ratifications among men than these. If the testimony (though it be of two men, but much more of three) of a seal or earnest is sufficient confirmation unto men, how much

Laurence Chaderton (1536–1640)

The first master of Emmanuel College at Cambridge University and tutor of William Perkins.

more certain is the testimony, seal, and earnest of the Spirit of God unto us?

Third, that which God offers and gives us particularly, we must receive particularly. But God offers and gives us Christ and all His benefits particularly in the Word and sacraments, and therefore we must have particular faith to receive Him. Some will say that they grant that we must receive Christ and His benefits in special, but that they do it by hope as the papists teach. I answer, it is a work of faith alone: "As many as received him…" (John 1:12). Who are the many? The next words show: "even they that believed on his name." Again, in the sacrament of the Supper, Christ is offered as the bread and water of life to everyone in particular; therefore, every believer must have something in his soul proportional to a hand and mouth, for receiving and feeding upon Him, which is nothing else but faith especially applying Christ and His benefits (John 6:35).

Fourth, the examples of believers in the Scriptures prove the same truth. Abraham believed by a particular faith: "it was imputed to him for righteousness" (Rom. 4:22). The same is true of Paul: "I live by the faith of the Son of God, who loved me, and gave himself for me" (Gal. 2:20). Now both these are patterns and precedents for us to follow: as they believed and particularly applied Christ to themselves, so must we (Rom. 4:24; 1 Tim. 1:16).

From these two, namely knowledge and application, follows confidence whereby we trust and rely upon Christ and His merits thus known and applied unto salvation. Because it inseparably follows faith, it is often in the Scriptures put for faith itself. But I distinguish it from faith. It has been said that it is a part of faith, but it is a fruit and follower of faith. The apostle manifestly distinguishes them: "In whom we have boldness and access with confidence by the faith of him" (Eph. 3:12).

The second point in this ground is the weight of it. That it is a main ground of religion appears in the following. (1) Paul says that if the inheritance of life is not by faith, it is not sure (Rom. 4:14). If we were entitled by works, the promise would not be certain. He then that rejects this ground of particular faith overthrows the gospel. (2) In the catechism of the primitive church, faith in God is made one ground (Heb. 6:1). (3) This ground is the main promise of the gospel; therefore, whoever overthrows it deprives men of all comfort of religion.

The adversaries of this ground are the common people who for the most part profess that they are not certain of the pardon of their sins. They hope well because God is merciful, but they think it is impossible to be certain, as though there can be hope and confidence where there is not assurance; but special hope always presupposes special faith.

15

Justification

Therefore we conclude that a man is justified by faith without the deeds of the law.
—Romans 3:28

To understand the meaning of this verse, we must know three things.[1] First, we must know what it is to be justified. In justification there are three distinct actions of God. (1) There is the freeing of a sinner from his sins for the merits of Christ. "And by him all that believe are justified from all things, from which ye could not be justified by the law of Moses" (Acts 13:39)—that is, acquitted from them. Paul describes it as the opposite of condemnation (Rom. 8:33), which is nothing else but a binding of a man to just punishment. (2) There is the reputing and accepting of a sinner as just for the merit of Christ. "Woe unto them...which justify the wicked" (Isa. 5:22–23)—that is, not to make but accept him just. "Wisdom is justified of all her children" (Luke 7:35)—that is, approved and acknowledged. (3) There is the acceptance of a sinner to life everlasting in Christ. After God has absolved a sinner and reputed him as just, there must follow this acceptance to life, which is therefore called "justification of life" (Rom. 5:18). The reason it is called this is rendered in the same

---

1. *Exposition of Jude*, 61–64.

place, for just as Adam's sin is imputed unto all, by which death entered, so Christ's obedience is imputed to believers thereby bringing life and justification.

From these three actions we may gather a true description of justification, to wit, it is an action of God the Father, absolving a sinner from all his sins, for the merit of Christ, accounting him as just, and accepting him to life everlasting.

Second, we must know what it is to be justified by faith. For the clear understanding of this weighty point, we must answer two questions. First, what is the very thing for which a sinner is justified? It is the obedience of Christ, the Redeemer and Mediator, passive and active. The former stands in suffering the death of His body and the pains of the second death in His soul, and the latter stands in fulfilling the law. The truth of this answer appears thus: since our fall we owe to God a double debt, we break the law and are bound to make satisfaction; and as creatures we must fulfill the rigor of the law and perform what it requires. Since we are bankrupt and unable to pay either parcel of this debt, we flee to our surety who must pay both for us. The former He does by His death, being "made a curse for us," and so "redeemed us from the curse" (Gal. 3:13). The latter He does by His perfect obedience unto the law, so that in Him we, doing these things, might "live in them" (v. 12).

The second question is this: seeing the obedience of Christ is the matter of our justification and is outside of ourselves, how is it made ours? First, to make it ours, God must give it to us. He does so when He gives us Christ Himself, for it is given with Him, and it is made ours when God in mercy esteems, judges, and accounts it to be ours, for it is ours by imputation. This appears by these two reasons. (1) As Christ is made our sin, so we are made His righteousness (2 Cor. 5:21). But He is made our sin by imputation and, therefore, His justice, being inherent to Him, is made ours by imputation. (2) As the first Adam's disobedience is made ours, so Christ's (the second Adam's) obedience is made ours (Rom. 5:17–18). But that is ours by imputation; therefore, it is also Christ's obedience. Second, to make this obedience ours, we must receive it, and that can be only by faith, which is the hand of the soul receiving into it the things that are given us by God. We must note, by the way, that a sinner is not justified by the dignity of his faith, but as it is an instrument whereby Christ's obedience is applied unto the soul.

Third, we must know what works are to be excluded from justification. The works of the moral and ceremonial law, works of nature and grace. That even works of grace are excluded appears by these reasons. (1) A sinner must so be justified that all cause of "boasting" is cut off (Rom. 3:27). But if a man were justified by works of grace, he would still boast—even if he acknowledged the works to be of God.[2] (2) If a man were justified by the works of the law, then his justification would stand "by the law." But if it did, the promise would be made void (Rom. 4:14). The tenor of that whole chapter proves that Abraham, having a supply of good works, was yet justified by faith without the works of the law. The objection in Romans 6:1 also witnesses to this

---

2. Perkins points to the example of the Pharisees in Luke 18.

truth: "What shall we say then? Shall we continue in sin that grace may abound?" It arises out of the first five chapters thus: if a man is justified by faith without works, we may continue in sin. But this objection would not have been an objection if it had not been the apostle's intent to prove justification by faith alone, without the works of the law. (3) Paul was not justified by any works: "I know nothing by myself; yet am I not hereby justified" (1 Cor. 4:4). Here he notes two things about himself: first, he had a good conscience within him; and, second, he was not thereby justified. In this way he debars all works of grace. (4) We are saved by grace without works. These excluded works are works of grace, for they are those which God has prepared for us to walk in (Eph. 2:8). (5) A man must first be justified before he can do a good work; therefore, works follow justification and cannot cause it.

As all works are excluded, so all virtues (except faith) are rejected. As in a man who stands to receive a gift, no part does anything to receive it but the hand, yet having received it, all other parts testify thankfulness, the tongue, the feet, and all the body, even so we receive the matter of our justification by faith alone, not by hope or love, but after receiving Christ, these with the other graces work and show themselves.

The second point in this ground is the weight of it, appearing herein, that he who overthrows it overturns the faith: "If they which are of the law be heirs, faith is made void, and the promise made of none effect" (Rom. 4:14). "If righteousness come by the law, then Christ is dead in vain" (Gal. 2:21).

16

Regeneration

Except a man be born of water and of the Spirit, he cannot enter into the kingdom of God.
—John 3:5

What is it to be born again?[1] There must be in him who is born again three things. The first is a real change from one estate to another. The change is when a mere natural man is made a new man, not in regard of his body or soul, or their powers, all of which a man retains after his regeneration, but in regard of God's image restored and renewed by Christ. This is the restoring of that new quality of righteousness and holiness, which was lost in Adam, as the apostle describes in Ephesians 4:24.

This change is attributed to "water" and the "Spirit" (John 3:5). By "water," our Savior alludes to some parts of the Old Testament, such as Ezekiel 36:25, where the prophet speaks of the cleansing of the church by sprinkling "clean water" upon it—that is, infusing new graces into the heart, which take place of the old corruption. By the "Spirit," Christ shows that this cleansing is by the inward working of the Holy Spirit.

---

1. *Exposition of Jude*, 64–66.

Some will say that if a man is a new man, then he must have a new soul. I answer, this new quality of righteousness and holiness is as it were a new soul, for in a regenerate man there is a body, a soul, and the Holy Spirit, which is the grace of sanctification opposed to flesh and corruption of nature (Rom. 8:10). This is as it were the soul of a soul renewed.

The second thing that must be in him who is born again is a root from whence this change may arise. This root is none other than Christ crucified, the Redeemer and Mediator, of whose body believers are members, of His flesh and bones (Eph. 5:30). As Eve was made of the side of Adam, so is every believer of the blood of Christ. And as every man, so far as he is a sinful man, springs from the first Adam, so every man, so far as he is renewed, springs from the second Adam, Christ Jesus. Now that a man may spring out of Christ, he must first, being taken out of the wild olive the old Adam (Rom. 6:5), be set and engrafted into the second Adam as a new stock, and that by faith wrought in the heart by the Spirit of God. By this incision he receives two things from Christ: first, in regard of his soul, holiness; and, second, in regard of his body, incorruption. Seeing that the whole man is united to Christ, both soul and body receive immortality and glory.

The third thing that must be in him who is born again is a new life, by which if any live not, he is not born again. For the distinct knowledge of this life, we must distinguish between uncreated life and created life. Uncreated life is the life of God, yea, God Himself, of which kind this is not. Created life is either natural or spiritual. Natural is that which we live by natural means, as food, drink, sleep, etc., of which kind this new life is not. But this is that spiritual life whereby a man in this life is ruled by the Spirit of God according to the Word. It stands in two things: first, the Spirit dwells in the heart; and, second, the Spirit rules over the heart. More plainly, this life has two degrees: first, when a man begins to savor, affect, and will spiritual things, loves them, and chiefly affects them when they have some savor and relish unto him (Rom. 8:5); and, second, when a man in all estates lives by a justifying faith, and orders his life thereby. The just man "shall live by his faith" (Hab. 2:4). This is, as it is truly called, "life eternal"—the beginning and first degree of which every believer possesses, even in this life.

The second point in this ground is the weight of it. Observe the necessity of the new birth in the former words where it is said that without it a man "cannot enter into the kingdom of God" (John 3:5). No man is in Christ who is not a "new creature" (2 Cor. 5:17). No man can come to God, unless he is a "new creature" (Gal. 6:15). It is a constant truth of Christ: "If I wash thee not, thou hast no part with me" (John 13:8).

17

Christian Liberty

Stand fast therefore in the liberty wherewith Christ hath made us free, and be not entangled again with the yoke of bondage.
—Galatians 5:1

Christian liberty is a spiritual right or condition, lost by Adam and restored by Christ.[1] I say "spiritual" because it pertains to the conscience. The use indeed of our liberty is in outward things, such as food, drink, apparel, etc., but the liberty itself is in the conscience. Thus, it differs from civil liberty, which stands in the moving of the body, in the choice of bodily actions, and in the free use of our goods. Christian liberty has two parts: a deliverance from misery and a freedom in good things.

Deliverance from misery has four parts. The first is a deliverance from the curse of the law for the breach thereof. "There is therefore now no condemnation to them which are in Christ Jesus" (Rom. 8:1). This comes to pass because there is a translation made of the curse from our persons to the person of Christ (Gal. 3:13). The second part is a deliverance from the obligation of the law. It binds us to bring perfect righteousness in our own persons for the

---

1. *Commentary on Galatians*, 318–20.

attainment of everlasting life, according to the tenor thereof: "Do this, and live." Deliverance from this obligation is procured because there is a translation made of the fulfilling of the law from our persons to the person of our Savior Christ.

From these two deliverances arise the pacification of the conscience, partly for our justification and partly for our conversation.

Touching justification, a sinner in his humiliation and conversion has by this doctrine a liberty, without respect to his own works or to his own fulfilling of the law, to rest on the mere mercy of God for the forgiveness of his sins and the salvation of his soul, and to appeal from the throne of divine justice to the throne of grace, and to oppose the merit of Christ against the wrath and judgment of God. This has always been the help of the godly in their distress (2 Chron. 33; Ezra 9; Dan. 9; Pss. 32; 51; 130; 143). Consider the example of the publican and the prodigal son who condemn themselves and make their appeal to the court of mercy and grace.

Here someone might ask: How will I know that I am freed from the rigor of the law and from the curse thereof? I answer, you must first set yourself at the bar of God's judgment. There you must arraign, accuse, and condemn yourself. This done, you must use your liberty and make your appeal to God's mercy and grace for pardon by asking, seeking, and knocking. Thus, at length you will be resolved touching your deliverance.

Touching conversation, our consciences are settled, in that we are freed from the rigor of the law because God in mercy accepts the will and endeavor

Christian Liberty

to believe, repent, and obey, for faith, repentance, and obedience. He spares those who fear Him, as a father spares his child when he endeavors to do what he can (Mal. 3:17). The law requires perfect obedience at our hands, yet God of His mercy looks more at the will to obey than the perfection of obedience. This must be a stay to our minds when we see more corruption than grace in ourselves and our obedience tainted with many spots of disobedience.

The third part of deliverance from misery is deliverance from the observation of the ceremonial law of Moses (Col. 2:16). Hence arises another deliverance from the bondage of human tradition, as Paul says, "Wherefore if ye be dead with Christ from the rudiments of the world, why, as though living in the world, are ye subject to ordinances?" (Col. 2:20). The fourth part of deliverance is from the tyranny and dominion of sin. "For sin shall not have dominion over you: for ye are not under the law, but under grace" (Rom. 6:14). In the conversion of the sinner, original sin receives its deadly wound, and the dominion thereof is diminished according to the measure of grace received.

The second part of Christian liberty is a freedom in good things. It is fourfold. The first is a freedom in the voluntary service of God. We are delivered "out of the hand of our enemies," that we "might serve him without fear, in holiness and righteousness before him, all the days of our life" (Luke 1:74–75). Paul says that "the law is not made for a righteous man" (1 Tim. 1:9), because he is a law to himself and freely does good duties as if there were no law to bind him. The cause of this freedom is the gift and donation of the Spirit of God. Therefore, David prays, "Uphold me with thy free spirit" (Ps. 51:12). Paul says, "Where the Spirit of the Lord is, there is liberty" (2 Cor. 3:17). Again, "For the law of the Spirit of life in Christ Jesus hath made me free from the law of sin and death" (Rom. 8:2).

Some say that this freedom in the voluntary service of God is bondage, for Christ says, "Take my yoke upon you" (Matt. 11:29). We are, therefore, as bound to the obedience of the law of God as Adam was by creation; nay, more strictly by reason of our redemption by Christ. I answer, the more we are bound to obedience, the freer we are because the service of God is not bondage but perfect liberty.

The second freedom is the free use of all the creatures of God (Rom. 14:14). "Unto the pure all things are pure" (Titus 1:15). The reason is because the dominion over the creatures lost by Adam is restored by Christ (1 Cor. 3:22). Hence it is that Paul calls the forbidding of marriage and food, with obligation of conscience, "doctrines of devils" (1 Tim. 4:1).

The third freedom is the liberty to come to God the Father in the name of Christ, and in prayer to be heard (Rom. 5:2; Eph. 3:12). According to our natural condition, our sins are a wall of partition between us and God, causing us to flee from the presence of God. Although we cry unto God and fill heaven and earth with our cries, so long as we are in our sins, we are not heard by Him.

The fourth freedom is a liberty to enter heaven in the day of our death, Christ by His blood having made a way (Heb. 10:19).

18

The Power of the Keys

Whatsoever ye shall bind on earth shall be bound in heaven: and whatsoever ye shall loose on earth shall be loosed in heaven.

—Matthew 18:18

To know the meaning of this verse, we must handle two things: first, what is this power of binding and loosing; and, second, what is the ratification and efficacy of this power in the words "bound and loosed in heaven."[1] Concerning the first, this power of "binding and loosing" is that authority given by God to His church on earth whereby it pardons, or retains as unpardoned, the sins of men. Men's sins are "cords" which bind them (Prov. 5:22) and "chains of darkness" in which they are reserved unto damnation (2 Peter 2:4). Hence, when men's sins are pardoned, they are said to be loosed. This power is called "the keys of the kingdom of heaven" (Matt. 16:19), for men's sins are as locks (yea, bars and bolts), shutting upon them the doors of heaven. When the church pardons sins, the doors of heaven are said to be opened, and when it retains them, heaven is shut against the sinner. Indeed, pardon of sin is properly granted and given by God, but men are truly said to

---

1. *Exposition of Jude*, 67–70.

pardon and retain sin when ministerially they pronounce what God pardons or does not pardon.

It will be said that men upon earth know not whose sins God will pardon and whose He will not. I answer, it is possible for man to know whose sins God will pardon and whose He will not, for God has generally made known that He will remit the sins of all believers and repentant sinners but will retain the sins of those who go on in the same. Now, we may know particularly who repents and believes, for the tree is known by its fruit, according to which the church may pronounce a true sentence.

To know more distinctly what this power is, the parts of it are to be considered. It stands partly in the ministry of the Word and partly in the justification of the church upon earth.

The ministry of the Word is either public or private. The public ministry of the Word is called the preaching of it. It is an ordinance of God by which ministers are called to pronounce in the name of God pardon of sins to the penitent and condemnation to the obstinate.... The private ministry stands in two things: first, private admonition; and, second, private comfort. Private admonition is God's ordinance whereby the minister in God's name binds a man to judgment for his sin, unless he repents. This is how Peter dealt with Simon Magus (Acts 8:21–22). Private comfort is when, upon true repentance, the minister pronounces upon the believer pardon of sin without condition. When David confessed, "I have sinned" (2 Sam. 12:13), Nathan tells him his sins are forgiven.

Concerning the jurisdiction of the church, it is a power given by God to the church whereby it uses

The Power of the Keys

correction upon open sinners for their salvation, and it stands in excommunication and absolution. Excommunication is a sentence excluding open and obstinate sinners from the kingdom of God, and consequently from the society of the church, for this follows the former: "If he neglect to hear the church, let him be unto thee as an heathen man" (Matt. 18:17). Paul calls this sentence a giving up of a man "unto Satan" (1 Cor. 5:5)....

This power of the church differs from the power of the civil magistrate in four things. (1) The power of the church is ordered only by the Word, but civil power by other civil laws. (2) The former corrects only by voice in admonition, suspension, and excommunication; the latter by real and bodily punishments. (3) All spiritual correction, as excommunication itself, stands at the repentance of a sinner, and proceeds no further; but the punishments of civil power stay not at repentance, but proceed on even to the death of the malefactor (notwithstanding his repentance) if he is a man of death. (4) In the civil there are three degrees of proceeding: first, the knowledge of the cause; second, the giving of the sentence; and, third, the execution of the punishment. In the ecclesiastical the third degree belongs to God alone.

The second thing in the meaning of the verse is to know what the ratification of this power is, namely, to be "bound and loosed in heaven." When the church's judgment, following the judgment of God, acquits or condemns a sinner, God in heaven has done it already and ratifies it. In absolution (as also in the other) pardon of sin is, first, given in heaven. Then, the church pronounces this according to God's will. Then, God ratifies it thereupon in heaven and confirms it as sure as if on earth He had pronounced the pardon.

The weight of this ground appears in Matthew 16:18, where the main promise of the gospel for the establishment of the church is contained: "Upon this rock I will build my church; and the gates of hell shall not prevail against it." The ground of our assurance thereof is added in verse 19, "I will give unto thee the keys of the kingdom of heaven." This makes the church prevail against the gates of hell, because it opens and shuts heaven. Hereby the Word and sacraments are preserved from pollution and profanation, the souls of men pulled out of the snares of the devil, and God's kingdom set open unto them. If this power is taken away, there is no difference left between the kingdom of God and the kingdom of the devil.

19

The Church

And are built upon the foundation of the apostles and prophets, Jesus Christ himself being the chief corner stone.
—Ephesians 2:20

There is, has been, and ever will be, a church, outside of which there is no salvation.[1] This is an article of our faith and a main ground of religion. If there were a time when there was not a church of God, Christ would only sometimes be a Redeemer, a King, because there would be no people redeemed, nor subjects to rule by His Word and Spirit.

The church is a company of men, chosen to salvation, called, united to Christ, and admitted into everlasting fellowship with Him. This description is easily derived from Hebrews 12:23 and 1 Peter 2:9. The church possesses six properties. (1) As the spouse of Christ, she is one, although distinguished in regard of time, as the church of the Old Testament and the New Testament, in regard of place, as of England, Scotland, etc., and in regard of condition, as the church militant and triumphant. All these make but one body of Christ. (2) It is invisible, not to be seen but believed, for election, vocation, and

---

1. *Exposition of Jude*, 71–72.

redemption can only be believed. Some parts of it are visible, such as the right use of the Word and sacraments. (3) All the promises of this life, and the life to come, especially forgiveness of sins and life everlasting, belong to this assembly and none other. (4) It consists of living members, quickened by the Spirit of Christ, not of any hypocrites or wicked persons. (5) No member of the church can be severed or cut off from Christ. Each member abides in Him and with Him forever. (6) It is the ground and pillar of truth, that is, the doctrine of true religion is always safely kept and maintained in it.

Some object that the churches on earth are true churches, yet they contain many hypocrites and apostates who fall from their profession; therefore, they are not all living members. I answer, there are two sorts of men in visible churches: just and hypocrites. Although hypocrites are within the church, yet the church is not so called on their account, but in regard of those who are truly joined to Christ (the better part)—even as a heap of wheat and chaff together is called a heap of wheat (the better part).

Adversaries of this ground include the papists who frame not the church by these true properties, but by deceitful marks such as succession, multitude, antiquity, and consent. When the church began, the first three of these did not exist, yet there was a true church.... The true mark of the church is the doctrine of the prophets and apostles truly taught and believed. A note of Christ's sheep is the hearing of His voice (John 10:27). "If that which ye have heard from the beginning shall remain in you, ye also shall continue in the Son, and in the Father" (1 John 2:24).

20

The Resurrection

For as in Adam all die, even so in Christ shall all be made alive.
—1 Corinthians 15:22

There will be a resurrection of the dead at the end of the world.[1] There are many arguments that prove there is a resurrection of the body after death, but I will only touch on the principal among them. The first is taken from the work of redemption. John says that Christ came to "destroy the works of the devil" (1 John 3:8). These works include sin and death by sin. Hence, I reason that, if sin and death will be dissolved utterly, then the bodies of the faithful, which are dead in the grave, must be made alive. Otherwise, death is not abolished. Sin and death must be utterly abolished; therefore, there will be a resurrection.

The second argument is taken from the covenant God made with His church: "I…will be their God, and they shall be my people" (Jer. 31:33). This covenant is not for a day or an age or a thousand years or ages, but it is everlasting and without end. God's people may say of God, "God is our God forever." Likewise, God will say of His church forevermore, "This people is My people." Now, if God's covenant

---

1. *An Exposition of the Symbol*, 398–400.

is everlasting, then all the faithful, departed from the beginning of the world, must be raised again to life. If God were to leave His people in the grave under death forever, how could they be called the people of God? He is a God of mercy and of life itself; therefore, although they abide long in the earth, they must at length be revived again. Christ uses this argument against the Sadducees, who denied the resurrection: "God is not the God of the dead, but of the living" (Matt. 22:32). But God is the God of Abraham, Isaac, and Jacob, who are dead; therefore, they must rise again.

The third argument is taken from the tenor of God's justice. It is a special part of God's glory to show forth His mercy upon the godly and His justice upon the wicked in rewarding them according to their works, as the apostle says, God "will render to every man according to his deeds: to them who by patient continuance in well doing seek for glory and honour and immortality, eternal life: but unto them that are contentious, and do not obey the truth, but obey unrighteousness, indignation and wrath" (Rom. 2:6–8). But, in this life, God does not reward men according to their doings. For this reason, Solomon, speaking of the estate of all men in this world, says, "All things come alike to all: there is one event to the righteous, and to the wicked; to the good and to the clean, and to the unclean; to him that sacrificeth, and to him that sacrificeth not" (Eccl. 9:2). Here the wicked flourish, while the godly are afflicted. The ungodly have their hearts' ease and all things at will, whereas the godly are oppressed and overwhelmed with all kinds of miseries and are as sheep appointed for the slaughter. It remains, therefore, that there must be a general resurrection of all men after this life, so that the righteous may obtain a reward of God's free mercy, and the wicked utter shame and confusion.

Some will say that it is sufficient for God to do this to the soul of every man, but the body does not need to rise again. I answer, the ungodly man does not work wickedness only in his soul, but his body is also an instrument thereof. And the godly man practices righteousness not only in his soul, but in his body also. The bodies of the wicked are the instruments of sin, and the bodies of the righteous are the weapons of righteousness. Therefore, their bodies must rise again, so that in both body and soul they may receive a reward, according to that which they have wrought in them.

The fourth argument, which is also used by Paul, is this: Christ "rose from the dead" (1 Cor. 15:12) and, therefore, all the faithful will rise again. He rose not for Himself as a private man, but in our room and stead and for us. If the Head is risen, then the members will also rise again, for by the same power whereby Christ raised Himself, He both can and will raise all those who are members of His mystical body. He is "the firstfruits of them that slept" (v. 20).

The fifth argument is taken from the express testimony of Scripture. Job declares, "For I know that my redeemer liveth, and that he shall stand at the latter day upon the earth: And though after my skin worms destroy this body, yet in my flesh shall I see God: Whom I shall see for myself, and mine eyes shall behold, and not another" (Job 19:25–27). Paul avouches and proves this point with sundry arguments in 1 Corinthians 15. "If the dead rise not... your faith is vain...they also which are fallen asleep in Christ are perished" (vv. 16–18).

The sixth argument is taken from the order of nature, which furnishes certain resemblances of the resurrection. Although they are not sufficient proofs, they are inducements to the truth.... Swallows, worms, and flies, which have been dormant in the winter season, in the spring, by the virtue of the sun's heat, revive again. Likewise, men fall in swoons and trances, being for a time without breath or sign of life, but afterward they come again. And (to use Paul's example) before the corn can grow and bear fruit, it must first be cast into the ground and rot (John 12:24). If this were not seen by experience, men would not believe it. Again, every present day is as it were dead and buried in the night following, yet it returns the next morning.

The last argument is that we read that the old prophets raised some from death, and that our Savior Christ raised Lazarus, among the rest, who had laid four days in the grave and stank. Why then should anyone think it impossible for God to raise all men to life?

21

The Judgment

The Lord Jesus Christ…shall judge the quick and the dead at his appearing and his kingdom.
—2 Timothy 4:1

There will be a general judgment of all flesh.[1] And you be as chaff that passes on a day (see Zeph. 2:2). The metaphor which the prophet uses is this: he compares the Lord to a great and rich husbandman. The whole world is His cornfield. The nations are His heaps of corn, but these heaps are full of chaff, that is, these particular churches are full of hypocrites. Now a wise husbandman lets the corn and chaff lie together until the wind blows; then he appoints his fanning time to separate the corn from the chaff, and to blow away the chaff. Likewise, God, the great and wise husbandman, will not let the chaff lie forever among the wheat. He has appointed His fanning times when He will blow the chaff into hell and gather His wheat into heavenly garners.

God's winnowing times are two. One is at the last day, after this life. It is God's great winnowing day of all His corn (that is, of all men), when the bad will be separated from the good forever, never to be mingled

---

1. "A Faithful and Plain Exposition Upon the Two First Verses of the Second Chapter of Zephaniah," in *Works* (1631), 3:424–25.

again with them. By the strong, powerful fan of His last and final judgment, He will blow them into hell. On that day, the wind of His wrath will be stronger than all the wind in the world.

God's other fanning time is in this world, and it is twofold. First, the preaching of the Word is one of God's fans. When the gospel is preached to a nation or congregation, it fans them, tries them, purges them, and so separates them, so that a man can see the manifest difference between the chaff and the wheat—that is, between the godly and the wicked. John the Baptist refers to this preaching of the gospel as a fanning. He says that Christ's fan is in His hand, and He will thoroughly purge His floor and gather His wheat into His garner, but He will burn the chaff with unquenchable fire (Matt. 3:12). The wind from this fan of the preached Word is so strong that it separates the chaff from the wheat—that is, good professors from hypocrites in the visible church. It blows so strongly upon the wicked that it brings them to the beginning of hell even in this world, as it works upon the conscience. Since it cannot convert them, it strikes them with fear, terror, and torment, either in life or at death. This torment of conscience is the very flash of hell fire.

When this first fan of the Word will not serve to bring men to repentance (for the Word preached does not actually confound a man, but only pronounces the sentence thereby striking the conscience), then God has another fan—the fan of His judgment. This fanning or winnowing time is when He executes His vengeance and His judgments on a nation. This is the latter fan, when the first will not prevail. It is His

The Judgment

powerful and strong fan driven about by the wind of His wrath. This fan went over the old world, and swept them all away, and went over the nation of the Jews, and we see they are no more.

These three fans of God make a threefold separation of the chaff from the wheat—that is, of the wicked from the elect. With the fan of His preached Word, which is powerful, He separates them in affection and disposition and makes a distinction between them, so as generally the wheat is known to be wheat and the chaff discerned to be chaff. Although the tares are known to be tares, both grow together, so that the Word only separates them in affection and sets several notes of distinction upon them both.

The second fan of His judgment is more violent, for thereby He separates them asunder in soul, gathering the souls of the godly as His wheat into heaven, and blowing the souls of the wicked into hell. Their bodies lie together, as partakers of the same judgment, so subject to the same corruption, and are lodged in the same grave of the earth, and death has like dominion over them all.

The third fan is God's great harvest and great winnowing time at the last day. With the wind of His power, He will sever them asunder in soul and body. He will separate the wheat from the chaff, the sheep from the goats. They will never be mingled again. And then with the wind of His wrath He will blow the chaff into unquenchable fire, and with His loving favor He will gather His wheat into the everlasting and glorious garners of heaven.

Christ's College, Cambridge

The school where William Perkins earned his degrees and later taught as a fellow.

SECTION TWO

Love: Grounds of Doctrine to Be Practiced

22

Repentance

Except ye repent, ye shall all likewise perish.
—Luke 13:3

Concerning repentance, two things must be taught: first, what it is; and, second, what is its use.[1] For the first, repentance (as Paul describes it) is a conversion whereby a sinner turns himself unto God and does "works meet for repentance" (Acts 26:20). There are two kinds of conversion of a sinner: first, that whereby God turns man; and, second, that whereby a man, being turned by God turns himself by grace. The former is not repentance properly, but the latter is. "Turn thou me, and I shall be turned.... Surely after that I was turned, I repented" (Jer. 31:18–19).

Conversion begins in the mind, but it is of the whole man, the mind laying off all purpose of sinning, the conscience calling back from sin, the will not seeking to fulfill the lusts of it; but the whole man endeavoring to please God through his whole conversation. Further, repentance is attended with divers fruits, worthy of newness of life. These are the duties of the moral law, performed in faith and truth without hypocrisy. Because they proceed from

---

1. *Exposition of Jude*, 72–74.

the same beginning, they are approved of God as repentance is.

The second point in this duty is the use of repentance. It is not a cause of salvation but only a way wherein men must walk to everlasting life. We are slandered by the popish church, for they claim that our doctrine requires nothing but faith to be saved, and so we become enemies to all good works. But this is not our doctrine, for we hold the works of repentance to be the way of salvation. Indeed, when we speak of the instrument whereby we lay hold upon Christ, we say faith alone, not hope, love, or any works; but when we speak of a way to life, then faith is not alone, but repentance is required, hope, the fear of God, and every good work…. Thus, Abraham's faith and works went together (James 2:22).

The adversaries of this ground are, first, professors of religion who content themselves with a feigned repentance, for most men being pricked and stung with the sense of their sins, for a while will hold down their heads like a bulrush, break off their company, come to church, pray, hear the Word, and perform other duties. But once the memory is past, they return to their former course of licentiousness. They think that this is a sufficient repentance, but it is merely ceremonial. It is like a fig leaf whereby men seek to cover themselves. True repentance changes the mind, will, affections, conscience, and all the actions of life.

The Roman Church is also an enemy of this ground. For hundreds of years, it has overturned this doctrine. First, they accept penance and public confession as repentance…. Second, they turn repentance into a judicial proceeding and a sentence of the court, in which the minister must be the judge, the sinner must come under confession, the minister must pass sentence, and the sinner must make satisfaction accordingly.... Third, they hold that the works of contrition, confession, and satisfaction, merit and confer the pardon of sin, and thereby they abolish the merit and satisfaction of Christ.

The Roman Church has deceived the world in various particulars concerning this doctrine. First, it teaches that repentance, for the original of it, is partly from nature, partly from grace, partly from God, partly from ourselves, which is a false foundation, joining light with darkness. Repentance is wholly from grace. Second, it makes remorse of conscience (which the very devils may have) a part of repentance. Saul, and even Judas, experienced this kind of contrition, which is no grace but a preparation unto it. Third, they make auricular confession, whereby every man is bound to confess each of his sins in the priest's ear, necessary unto repentance. They say that without this there is no pardon. This is a very gallows to the conscience. Fourth, they turn their canonical satisfaction into satisfaction of God's justice for sin, wherein blasphemously they overthrow the most perfect satisfaction of the Son of God. We are, therefore, to praise God who has taken from our necks this yoke of the Roman Church, which neither we nor our fathers were able to bear.

23

Self-Denial

If any man will come after me, let him deny himself, and take up his cross daily, and follow me.
—Luke 9:23

We will consider three things: first, the meaning; second, the moment; and, third, the adversaries against whom we must contend.[1] For the meaning, "If any man will come after me"—that is, "will be My disciple" (for disciples used to follow their masters and teachers)—he must learn three duties.

The first duty is to deny ourselves, which requires three things. (1) We must, for the magnifying of the grace of God, abase ourselves even to nothing. We have an example of this in Paul: "I have planted, Apollos watered; but God gave the increase. So that neither is he that planteth anything, neither he that watereth; but God that giveth the increase" (1 Cor. 3:6–7). If the planter is nothing, much less is the planted. Of ourselves, we are not able to think a good thought. "Our sufficiency is of God" (2 Cor. 3:5). (2) We must renounce our own reason and will, bringing them under subjection to the will of God. We must not strive to have wills of our own but let Christ's will be sufficient for us. His wisdom must be

---

1. *Exposition of Jude*, 74–76.

our reason. (3) We must esteem all things as dung for Christ, and preserve within us a readiness to leave and forsake friends, riches, honors, yea, our liberty and life itself (if need be), for His sake and a good conscience.

The second duty is to take up our cross daily, which requires two things. (1) Every member of the church must reckon of and look for daily crosses in his calling and in his profession. (2) When the cross comes, it must be taken up cheerfully and borne with rejoicing: "Rejoice, and be exceeding glad" even when men "revile" and "persecute" you (Matt. 5:11–12). Justified persons are able to "glory in tribulations" (Rom. 5:3), according to the exhortation, "count it all joy" (James 1:2), and according to the example of the saints who "took joyfully the spoiling of [their] goods" (Heb. 10:34).

The third duty is to follow Christ. When Christ says, "follow me," it is as though He says, "I go before you, bearing My cross, let My disciples follow Me step by step in bearing this cross." This contains the main duties of Christian religion. (1) We must bear the cross in obedience, as Christ did, who most willingly abased Himself to death, even the death of the cross, in obedience to His Father's will. Christ's obedience included the practice of three special virtues. The first was meekness. He opened not His mouth; He reviled not when He was reviled; He avenged not when He might. The second was patience. He grudged not to suffer those bitter torments for His very enemies. The third was love. He prayed for those who pierced Him, and He shed His heart blood for them. In all of this, it is our part

Self-Denial

to imitate Him. (2) We must be conformable unto Christ, our Head. This consists in crucifying our body of corruption, even as He was crucified upon His cross. We must arm ourselves with Peter's exhortation to suffer in the flesh as Christ suffered in the flesh (1 Peter 4:1). Whoever does this "hath ceased from sin." He does not live "to the lusts of men, but to the will of God" (v. 2). The learning of this duty helps forward our obedience under the cross, which many cannot attain unto because they bear not about in their bodies the "dying of the Lord Jesus" (2 Cor. 4:10).

The moment and weight of this ground appears in Luke 9:24, "For whosoever will save his life shall lose it"—that is, he, who refuses to take up his cross to follow Christ, will never be saved. Again, baptism is a main ground (Heb. 6:1), namely, as it is joined with inward baptism...especially in regard of that stipulation we make, and that profession which we receive upon us thereby, of forsaking ourselves and following Christ, without which there is no salvation....

The adversaries are, first, among ourselves, such as are content to make Christ a Savior and Redeemer but not a pattern and example of imitation in His virtues. Christ will not be made a packhorse only to bear sins, seeing He has propounded Himself as a precedent to be followed by those who look for salvation by His sufferings. They must first be His disciples before He is their Redeemer. Second, a more wicked enemy withstanding this doctrine is the Church of Rome, in exalting nature and extenuating the grace of God. (1) It holds that not all sins deserve death, but they may be done away with by a little knocking on the breast or such light sorrow. (2) It holds that man by nature has free will in his conversion, and being helped by the Holy Spirit, can move himself unto salvation. (3) It holds that after justification there is nothing in a man that God can hate. (4) It holds that a man may merit life and perform works of satisfaction to God. These devilish doctrines make the heart swell with pride, so as it can never be brought to the denial of itself.

24

Choosing God

Thou shalt have no other gods before me.
—Exodus 20:3

The first table of the law contains four commandments.[1] The first teaches us to have and choose the true God for our God.... We must choose Jehovah to be our God. The duties here commanded are these. (1) We must acknowledge God, that is, know and confess Him to be such a God as He has revealed Himself to be in His Word and creatures (Jer. 24:7; Col. 1:10). We must glory in this knowledge of God (Jer. 9:24). (2) We must seek union with God, whereby we are knit in heart with Him (Josh. 23:8; Acts 11:23). Man cleaves unto God in three ways.

The first is faith, whereby a man, acknowledging the power and mercy of God, steadfastly rests in Him against all assaults (2 Chron. 20:20; Ps. 27:1–3). Hence arises patience, and alacrity in present perils (Gen. 45:5; 2 Sam. 16:10; 2 Kings 6:16; Ps. 39:9). This faith engenders hope, which is a patient expectation of God's presence and assistance in all things that are to come (Ps. 37:5–7; Prov. 16:3).

The second is love, whereby a man, acknowledging God's goodness and favor toward Him, loves

---

1. *Golden Chain*, in *Works* (1631), 1:32–34.

Him above all things (Deut. 6:5). The marks of the true love of God are these: (1) to hear willingly His Word; (2) to speak often of Him; (3) to think often of Him; (4) to do His will without irksomeness; (5) to give body and all for His cause; (6) to desire His presence above all and to bewail His absence; (7) to embrace all such things as appertain to Him; (8) to love and hate that which He loves and hates; (9) to seek to please Him in all things; (10) to draw others unto the love of Him; (11) to esteem highly of such gifts and graces as He bestows; (12) to stay ourselves upon His counsels revealed in His Word; and (13) to call upon His name with faith.

The third is fear, whereby a man, acknowledging both God's mercy and justice, fears to displease God because it is the greatest evil (Pss. 4:4; 130:4; Hab. 3:16). From this arises the godly man's desire to approve himself in all things to his God (Gen. 5:22; 17:1).

Out of these three virtues proceeds humility, whereby a man, acknowledging God's free bounty and prostrating himself before Him, ascribes to Him all praise and glory (1 Chron. 29:10–11, 14; 1 Cor. 1:31; 1 Peter 5:5)....

This place forbids various sins. (1) It forbids ignorance of the true God and His will, which is not only not to know but also to doubt of such things as God has revealed in His Word (Jer. 4:22; 9:3). (2) It forbids atheism, when the heart denies either God or His attributes, such as His justice, wisdom, providence, or presence (Ps. 14:1; Mal. 1:2; 3:14; Eph. 2:12). (3) It forbids errors concerning God, the persons of the deity, or the attributes. Hellenism is here

James Montagu (1568–1618)

Bishop Montagu preached Perkins's funeral sermon. His text was from Joshua 1:2, "Moses my servant is dead."

reproved, for it acknowledges and adores a multiplicity of gods. Judaism is here condemned, for it worships one God without Christ. The same may be said of the heresies of Marcion who denied that God was the Creator of the world, Sabellius who denied the distinction of the three persons, and Arius who said that Christ, the Son of God, is not very God. (4) It forbids the withdrawal and removal of the affections of the heart from the Lord, and the setting of them upon other things (Isa. 29:13; Jer. 12:2).

25

Fleeing Idolatry

Thou shalt not make unto thee any graven image.
—Exodus 20:4

How may we keep ourselves from idols?[1] That we may thoroughly preserve ourselves from their contagion, we must do four things. First, we must avoid making them. "Thou shalt not make unto thee any graven image, or the likeness of anything." These words forbid images of all kinds, graven or painted, and images of all things in heaven, earth, and under the earth. Tertullian notes that John warns us to keep ourselves from idols, not merely idolatry—that is, we are to keep ourselves from the images themselves, not merely the use of them.

The simple making of images is not forbidden, for there is a lawful use of images. The first use is holy, when they serve to signify the holy things of God. Such images are properly signs and types, and they are appointed by God.... The second use is historical, when they serve to represent human or divine history. Here it must be remembered that the painting of the history of the Bible, though otherwise lawful, is not expedient in churches because of the danger of it giving rise to idolatry. Commendable is

---

1. *A Warning against Idolatry*, in *Works* (1631), 1:685–86.

the practice of the Church of England, which suffers not, in places that serve for the use of religion, either painted or carved images.... The third use is when images are made for the beautifying of houses, either public or private, that serve only for civil meetings.

It is the scope and intent of the commandment of God to forbid the making of images for divine or religious use, that is, to represent God in His nature or properties or presence. Some may object as follows: When we think of God, we conceive an internal image or form of Him in our minds, and that which we conceive we may proportionally set down by painting or carving. If the eternal form of God may be lawfully conceived, why cannot the external form be made? I answer, the right way to conceive God is not to conceive of any form but to conceive in mind His properties and proper effects. As soon as the mind frames unto itself any form of God (as when He is conceived to be an old man, sitting on a throne in heaven with a scepter in His hand), an idol is set up in the mind....

Second, we must avoid keeping idols—that is, images that have been abused to idolatry and are in likelihood still to be abused, especially if they stand in public places. The commandment of God is to destroy the idols of the heathen, their altars, and their high places. According to this commandment, Moses destroyed the golden calf, and Hezekiah the brazen serpent (Ex. 32:20; 34:13; Deut. 7:25; 2 Kings 18:4)....

Third, we must avoid using idols. The worship of idols is utterly condemned in the second part of the commandment: "Thou shalt not bow down thyself to them, nor serve them" (Ex. 20:5). In these words, the Lord identifies two parts in the worship of idols: honor and service. Honor is either inward in the affection of reverence or outward in the gestures of the body, as the removing of the hat, the raising of the hands and eyes, the bowing of the knees, the prostrating of the body, and such like. Likewise, service is either inward in the devotion of the mind, in confidence, hope, invocation, vows, and such like, or outward in all other duties that are beside the gesture of the body, as sacrifices, oblations, pilgrimages, burning incense, erecting altars, etc. All these are utterly forbidden.

Furthermore, that there may be no place for the use of idols among the people of God, He has by law straightly barred us the use of all such things as are properly memories and monuments of idols: "Make no mention of the name of other gods, neither let it be heard out of thy mouth" (Ex. 23:13). All things that pertain to the worship of idols must be eschewed. Upon this ground Paul argues that the Corinthians must not be present, or sit down, at the feasts which were made to the honor of heathen gods, even if they abstained from worshiping them (1 Cor. 10:14–33)....

Fourth, we must avoid those who use idols.... The idolaters of this last age paint over their idolatries and blear the eyes of the world. We have a special caveat given us by the Holy Spirit to beware of them. "Beware lest any man spoil you through philosophy and vain deceit, after the tradition of men" (Col. 2:8).

26

Worshiping God

Thou shalt worship the Lord thy God, and him only shalt thou serve.
—Matthew 4:10

Worship in general betokens the exhibiting and giving of reverence and honor to another.[1] This worship is twofold: civil or divine. Civil worship is that outward reverence and honor which one man gives to another by prostrating the body, bowing the knee, etc. The end of civil worship is to testify and acknowledge superiority and preeminence in another, either for authority and office, as the subject worships his king and governor, or for gifts and graces, or for old age, as inferiors in gifts and younger in age by due reverence must acknowledge. In this civil manner did Jacob bow himself seven times to his brother Esau, thereby acknowledging him as his superior and better (Gen. 33:3). Thus did Abraham bow himself before the Hittites (Gen. 23:7) and Lot unto the angels that came into Sodom (Gen. 19:1). In this civil manner it is lawful to kneel before kings

---

1. *Combat between Christ and the Devil*, in *Digest or Harmony of the Books of the Old and New Testaments; Combat Between Christ and the Devil; Sermon on the Mount*, ed. J. Stephen Yuille, in vol. 1 of *The Works of William Perkins*, gen. ed. Joel R. Beeke and Derek W. H. Thomas (Grand Rapids: Reformation Heritage Books, 2014), 151–54.

and princes, to testify our subjection unto them, and loyal acknowledgment of their preeminence over us under God.

Divine worship is the ascribing of divinity to the thing we honor, whereby we make it unto us some divine thing above the order of any creature. A man may ascribe divinity unto something in four ways: (1) by attributing the Godhead unto it, or giving unto it such honor whereby he acknowledges the same to be God; (2) by ascribing unto it the attributes of God, such as omnipresence, omnipotence, omniscience, etc.; (3) by accepting and acknowledging it to be the Creator and Governor of all things; and (4) by acknowledging it to be the Giver of all good things, the Defender and Deliverer from all evil. When a man ascribes any of these to a thing in worship, he ascribes divinity to that same thing. This divine worship principally consists in religion which indeed is God's worship, and piety whereby men ascribe unto a thing divine and religious honor.

Divine worship is twofold: inward in the mind or outward in the body. Inward divine worship is when a man gives his heart and soul to something, devoting the affections of his heart (love, fear, joy, hope, faith, and confidence) to it. He does so because he conceives it to be God, having divine properties such as omnipotence, wisdom, justice, mercy, etc., or he conceives it to be the Creator and Governor of all, or the Giver of all good things unto him, and his Preserver from all evil. This devotion of the heart and soul to God, with its faculties and affections, is the ground and substance of all divine worship, and indeed can be given to nothing but to that which is God or conceived to be God.

Outward divine worship is when a man bows, prostrates, or casts down his body to anything, thereby testifying that his mind and heart are devoted to it. He holds it to be God, to be omnipotent, etc., the Creator and Governor and Preserver, and therefore he reposes his trust and confidence therein, and he sets his love, joy, and fear thereon above all other things. Here we may observe a difference between civil worship and divine worship. By outward civil worship we only acknowledge preeminence and superiority in another in regard of authority, gifts, age, or such like. But by outward divine worship we acknowledge divinity to be in the thing before which we bow or prostrate ourselves. We must also remember that outward divine worship serves only to testify to inward divine worship, to make known what we conceive to be God and to what we have devoted the affections of our hearts....

Besides this worship, God mentions a serving of Him.... Service, in general, is nothing else but the giving and performing of obedience to the commandment of another. This service is twofold: absolute or partial. Absolute service is when a man obeys the commandment of another without any condition or exception, and not only outwardly in body, but in soul and conscience, in thought, will, and affection. This absolute service is proper to God alone, for we must never call His commandments into question, but look at what He commands, and since He commands it we simply and absolutely yield obedience to it, not only outwardly in body but inwardly in soul and spirit with the powers and faculties thereof, and in all the affections of our hearts.

Partial service is that which is due to governors and superiors from their inferiors in the Lord. God has given power to magistrates here on earth to make laws for the good of civil estates. Their inferiors must yield obedience to the laws, not absolutely but with restraint—that is, in the Lord, so far forth as their commands agree with His will and cross not His command. Again, our obedience unto them is in body and outward conversation. Indeed, we must from the heart yield service and obedience unto them, but yet the conscience properly cannot be bound by men's laws; they only concern the outward man in speech, gesture, and behavior.

Now of these two kinds of service, our Savior Christ speaks here of simple and absolute service, whereby both soul and body with all their powers and parts thereof yield absolute obedience and subjection to the will and commandment of God.

We see what worship and service are here required. Now we must observe the person to whom the same is to be given: "the Lord thy God." Divine worship, whether inward or outward, and absolute service of the whole man, must be given to no creature, angel or man, be they ever so excellent, but to the true God alone. The scope and drift of the first and second commandments are to bind every man to give so much to his God and to beware of giving the same to any other beside the Lord. And the practice of the good angel that talked with John shows the same thing, for when John fell before his feet to worship him, the angel said, "See thou do it not" (Rev.

19:10). Here we see that the good angels strive for the furtherance of God's right in these duties, but this wicked spirit, in tempting Christ, seeks God's great disgrace. Thus, we may perceive that Christ's application of this text against Satan's temptation is most pregnant. Christ justly repulsed Satan for requiring Him to prostrate His body before him in token that He did worship him as the giver of those kingdoms which he offered unto Him. This text binds every man to give outward divine worship, whereby the inward worship of the heart is signified, to God alone, and not to any creature.

27

Sanctifying God

Sanctify the LORD of hosts himself; and let him be your fear, and let him be your dread.
—Isaiah 8:13

These words contain the substance of the third commandment.[1] For the meaning, a thing is said to be sanctified in two ways: when it is made holy or when it is acknowledged to be holy. The latter sense must be understood here, for God's name (which is holiness itself and the first cause of all holiness) cannot be made holy. It is sanctified by us when we acknowledge it as holy. Our sanctification of God respects either God Himself or God's gifts. Our sanctification of God Himself (the thing intended in this ground) is done in two ways.

First, we sanctify God Himself when, in our mind, we acknowledge and praise Him in His attributes of wisdom, mercy, loving-kindness, power, providence, and such like. "Sanctify the Lord God in your hearts" (1 Peter 3:15)—that is, acknowledge Him in His wisdom, power, and other attributes. As good subjects, speaking of their prince, will put off their hats in reverent opinion of him, so we should religiously think and speak of these attributes. Job,

---

1. *Exposition of Jude*, 83–85.

suspecting that his sons in their feastings had dishonored God's name, sanctified them (Job 1:5). When Hezekiah heard the blasphemies of Rabshakeh against God, he humbled himself, rent his clothes, and put on sackcloth (2 Kings 19:1). Wicked Ahab, having heard (though falsely) that Naboth had blasphemed God, rent his clothes and proclaimed a fast, which shows (whatever his fast was) the use and manner of holy men in his time when God's name was dishonored and blasphemed.[2]

Second, we sanctify God Himself when we reverently acknowledge His titles, such as God, Lord, Jehovah, Father, Christ, Jesus, Holy Spirit, and not without religious and obedient affection speaking or thinking of them.

Our sanctification of God's gifts, which are many, as the preached Word, prayer, sacraments, food, drink, and all things that serve for the good of body or soul, is not done by giving or adding any holiness unto them (which in themselves are all holy), but by acknowledging them to be holy by preparing ourselves to a holy use of them, and using them accordingly with a good conscience. Every creature of God has a double use: (1) a lawful use, when God permits a general use of His creatures, thus all may use food, drink, apparel, etc.; and (2) a holy use, when a creature in its lawful use is used in a holy manner, for this includes the former, though that may be without this. For example, all

---

2. Perkins seems to have confused the details of this story. Ahab does not "rent his clothes" until confronted by the prophet Elijah. See 1 Kings 21:5–29.

William Ames (1576–1633)

Puritan theologian converted under the ministry of William Perkins. Ames wrote, "I gladly call to mind the time, when being young, I heard worthy Master Perkins, so preach in a great assembly of students, that he instructed them soundly in the truth, stirred them up effectually to seek after godliness, made them fit for the kingdom of God; and by his own example showed them, what things they should chiefly intend, that they might promote true religion, in the power of it, unto God's glory, and others' salvation."

the Jews kept the Passover lawfully, but only those celebrated it holily who prepared themselves according to the commandment. Our holy use of God's gifts is obtained by the Word and prayer (1 Tim. 4:5). The Word directs us to use these gifts in obedience, and prayer obtains grace to use them according to the Word.

We should be moved unto a holy use of God's creatures by these reasons. (1) We are different from the brute beasts. The swine in the forest eats up the fruit, but he does not look to heaven, not even to the tree from where it falls. (2) We have lost our title to all the creatures in Adam, which only is in this use restored. (3) They are the gifts of God. We acknowledge them to be His, and in Him learn to use them. (4) We avoid the common abuse of them whereby He is provoked to displeasure.

The second point is the weight of this ground, which may appear in the contrary, seeing blasphemers do what they can to overthrow the Godhead (Lev. 24:14–16). They are called by such a name as signifies "a piercer of God," or one who thrusts God through. Therefore, the sanctification of God is a ground of moment. Second, the first petition of the Lord's Prayer is "sanctified be Thy name." Here we are taught to prefer and pray for the hallowing of God's name before our own salvation. Third, the scope of the third commandment is the same, which whosoever observes not, reverses both the former. Fourth, the Lord is so jealous of His glory that He will be sanctified of all them that come near Him (Lev. 10:3), else He will sanctify Himself in their confusion.

28

Loving Our Neighbor

For all the law is fulfilled in one word, even in this;
Thou shalt love thy neighbor as thyself.
—Galatians 5:14

Church: Some teach that faith is sufficient, and they embolden us to live as we will.[1]

John: Little children, let no man deceive you. Whoever works righteousness is righteous as He is righteous. Whoever commits sin, though he says he believes, and therefore thinks himself justified before God, is of the devil, resembles the devil, as the child does the father, and is governed by his spirit. The devil sins from the beginning of the world. The Son of God was made manifest for this purpose, that He might dissolve the works (for the beginning and continuance of all rebellion and disobedience) of the devil. Further, to display these seducers, whoever is born of God sins not (he does not keep a course in sin) even though he might fall by infirmity, for His seed, or God's Word cast into the heart, by the operation of the Spirit making a man to spring into a new

---

1. *A Case of Conscience, the Greatest that Ever was: How a Man May Know whether He be a Child of God or No*, in *Works* (1631), 1:425–26.

creature, remains in him. Neither can he sin because he is born of God.

Church: Briefly, to come to the point, how may it be known who is God's child and who is to be reputed a child of the devil?

John: In this are the children of God known, and the children of the devil: whoever works not righteousness is not of God, neither, to give you a plain example, he who loves not his brother. This is the message which you have heard from the beginning, that we should love one another. Not as Cain. He was of the evil one, Satan, and slew his brother. Why slew he him? Because his own works were evil and his brother's good.

Church: Yet if we love those who are our brethren, according to the flesh, they cease not to hate and persecute us?

John: Marvel not my brethren that this world hates you.

Church: If not to love is a note of the child of the devil, what is the note of God's child?

John: We know that we are translated from death to life because we love the brethren…on the contrary, he who loves not his brother abides in death, or is under the state of damnation. Whoever hates his brother is a manslayer, and you know that no manslayer has eternal life abiding in him.

Church: You have shown us fully that love is a work of adoption. Now, show us how we may know whether we love our brethren or not.

John: He laid down His life for us. Therefore, we ought, carried with the like affection of love, to lay down our lives for the brethren.

Church: Many in speech do pretend love, but we find not this willing affection and readiness to show love.

John: Whoever has this world's goods, with which this life is sustained, and sees his brother has need, and shuts up his bowels or has no compassion…how dwells the love of God in him?

Church: What other note is there of true love?

John: My little children, let us not love in word nor in tongue only, but in deed and truth sincerely, for thereby we know that we are of the truth, sound professors of the gospel of Christ, and will before Him appease our hearts in regard of any accusation that our conscience will lay unto us before God's judgment seat. If our heart condemns us, an evil conscience accuses us, God is greater than our heart, namely, in judging us, and knows all things.

Church: How may we know that our consciences will not condemn us?

John: Beloved, if our hearts condemn us not, then we have boldness toward God, to come unto Him by prayer.

"The Wholesome Doctrine of the Gospel"

Church: What other fruit is there of true love?

John: Whatever we ask, we receive from Him because we keep His commandments, and do those things which are pleasant in His sight.

Church: What are those commandments?

John: This then is His commandment, that we believe in the name of His Son, Jesus Christ, and love one another as He commanded.

Church: Do those who keep these commandments prove this?

John: Yes, for whoever keeps His commandments dwells in Him, and He in him.

Church: How may we know that God dwells in us and we in Him?

John: Hereby we know that He abides in us, by that Spirit of sanctification whereby we are renewed, which He has given us.

29

Honoring Our Parents

Honour thy father and thy mother.
—Exodus 20:12

The son is he who is in subjection to his parents.[1] The duties of a son to be performed to his parents are principally two. First, he is to yield obedience to them, whether they are his natural parents or otherwise, as his stepfather and stepmother, and that while he lives (Ex. 18:19; Ruth 3:5; Luke 2:51; John 1:5; Eph. 6:1). This obedience must show itself in two things. (1) He is to obey in the choice of a lawful calling, wherein he is to be ordered and appointed at the discretion of the parent. (2) He is to obey in marriage, for the parent is the principal agent and disposer of the child. Although the parents' authority is not so great that the child is to be forced and compelled, yet the reverent and dutiful respect which the child ought to bear toward his parents ought to be a strong inducement, not to dissent or renounce their advice without great and weighty cause. The child must endeavor by all manner of dutiful carriage to overcome, or at least to mitigate, his parents' severity in that behalf.

---

1. *Oeconomie. Or, Household Government*, in *Works* (1631), 3:695–96.

Now, for daughters, they must yield obedience to their parents in all domestic labors, so that they may be skillful in household affairs. Thus did the seven daughters of the priest of Midian accustom themselves to draw water and fill the troughs to water their father's sheep (Ex. 2:16). Thus Rebekah was seen to come out of her father's house, with her pitcher upon her shoulder, and go down with it to the well to fill it, and give drink to her father's camels (Gen. 24:16–17).

The second duty of the son is to recompense his parents' love and care over him by relieving them in case of need, if God give ability, with food and raiment and other necessities. Herein children must deal with their parents as the brood of the stork is reported to do with her, by feeding her when she is old, wherein they do no more but what she before has done unto them. It is Paul's counsel that children and nephews should recompense the kindness of their kindred in the first place (1 Tim. 5:4) and therefore to their parents, the head and foundation of their kindred. When Joseph was in prosperity, his father Jacob in want, he first gave him corn freely, and afterwards sent for him to Egypt, and there provided for him, in so much as the text says of him that he nourished his father and his brethren, and all his father's household with bread, "even as a mother puts meat into the child's mouth" (Gen. 47:12). When Naomi, the stepmother of Ruth, was of great years and her strength spent, Ruth gathered corn in the harvest for the relief of them both. When Boaz gave her to eat and drink, she reserved part of it and brought it home with her gleanings to refresh her mother (Ruth 2:14, 18).

The necessity of the performance of these duties is so great that if the son neglects them, doing the contrary through the ill use of his parents, either in word or deed, he is worthy of death, even by Moses's law (Ex. 21:15).

30

Cultivating Virtue

He hath shewed thee, O man, what is good; and what doth the LORD require of thee, but to do justly, and to love mercy, and to walk humbly with thy God.
—Micah 6:8

Three virtues are here required: justice, mercy, and humility.[1] Touching the first, we are commanded to "do justly." This execution of justice between man and man has five substantial parts. (1) We give honor to whom honor is due. (2) We preserve the body and soul of our neighbor (that is, his spiritual and temporal life) by thought, word, and deed. (3) We guard his chastity, which is the honor of body and soul in single life and matrimony. (4) We guard his worldly estate. (5) We guard his good name. This is the scope of all the commandments of the second table.

Now, the due execution of justice must be tempered with mercy, which is a readiness to relieve the misery of the distressed. Because justice and mercy without godliness are but civil virtues, we are in the last place commanded to "walk in humility with our God." This contains the sum of the first table, and stands in three things: (1) we must acknowledge our sins; (2) we must entreat for pardon; and (3) we must

---

1. *Exposition of Jude*, 87–88.

purpose not to offend God any more but endeavor to prevent sin to come.

Concerning the weight of this ground, it appears in Micah 6:7, where the Lord testifies to be more delighted with the practice of love and mercy than with oblations of "thousands of rams" or "ten thousand of rivers of oil." Elsewhere, He declares, "I will have mercy, and not sacrifice." This is the end of the appearing of the grace of God, that we should live "soberly" in regard of ourselves, "justly" in regard of others, and "godly" in regard of God (Titus 2:12). These virtues are so respected by God that they are said to go immediately before His face (Ps. 89:14), and so necessary among men that no society can be preserved without them.

The adversaries hereof are the lives of most men who seek their own things, and do not maintain the lives, goods, name, or chastity of others. Too many prefer their private gain before the common good of men in church and commonwealth.

The main adversary is the Roman religion, which defends the greatest injustice by establishing a monarchy among themselves, not only controlling the sovereign authority of princes in their own kingdoms, but also exempting their subjects from their allegiance....

That religion overthrows justice in chastity. (1) It gives power to the pope to dispense with marriages within degrees of nature; it licenses the brother by that dispensation to marry his brother's wife, and so is a patron of horrible incest. (2) It defends the toleration of brothels. (3) It forbids marriages to sundry orders of men, which Paul calls a doctrine of

Queen Elizabeth (r. 1558–1603)

Perkins's life coincided with almost the entirety of Queen Elizabeth's reign.

devils (1 Tim. 4:1). It binds certain men and women from marriage, and yet calls it a sacrament. (4) The last Council of Trent affirms that all marriages not solemnized by a Mass priest and in the faith of the Roman Church are of none effect.

That religion teaches that to steal a small thing is a venial sin, whereas the thought of stealing deserves the curse of the law. It defends begging, yea, and places holiness in it, whereas the Word teaches that there should be no beggar in Israel (Deut. 15:4). It teaches that a sporting lie or a beneficial lie are venial sins, but this is flat against the ninth commandment. It teaches injustice, namely, that hurtful motions intended against our neighbor (if there is no consent of will) are not sin.

From all this, we see what to think of that religion. Christ tells us, "Whosoever therefore shall break one of these least commandments, and shall teach men so, he shall be called the least in the kingdom of heaven" (Matt. 5:19)—that is, he has no part therein. But the Roman Church breaks them and teaches men to do the same, and therefore it is not of God, and its peremptory teachers have no part (without repentance) in the kingdom of heaven.

31

Pursuing Our Calling

Let every man abide in the same calling wherein he was called.
—1 Corinthians 7:20

A vocation (calling) is a certain kind of life, ordained and imposed on man by God, for the common good.[1] First, I say it is a certain condition or kind of life; that is, a certain manner of leading our lives in this world. For example, the life of a king is to spend his time in the governing of his subjects, and that is his calling. The life of a subject is to live in obedience to the magistrate, and that is his calling. The state and condition of a minister is to lead his life in the preaching of the gospel and the Word of God, and that is his calling. A master of a family is to lead his life in the government of his family, and that is his calling. In a word, a calling is that particular and honest manner of life, to which every man is called and set apart....

God is the author of every calling and has two actions therein. First, He ordains the calling itself. Second, He imposes the calling on man. Therefore, I say vocation is a certain kind of life ordained and imposed by God. For the first, God ordains a calling when He prescribes and commands the same,

---

1. *A Treatise of Vocations*, in *Works* (1631), 1:750–51.

in and by His Word. And those callings or states of life, which have no warrant from God's Word, are unlawful. Now, God, in His Word, ordains callings in two ways: (1) by commanding and prescribing them particularly, as He does the most weighty callings in the family, church, or commonwealth; and (2) by appointing and setting down certain laws and commandments generally, whereby we may easily gather that He does either approve or not approve of them, though they are not particularly prescribed in the Word.

The second action of God, which is the imposition of callings, is when He particularly sets apart any man to any particular calling. This must be understood of all callings in the world. God does this in two ways. (1) He does it by Himself immediately, without the help of any creature. Adam was called and appointed to dress the garden of Eden. Abraham was called from the idolatry of his forefathers. Moses was called to be a prince over the Israelites and guide them out of Egypt into the promised land. In the New Testament, the apostles were called to preach the gospel. (2) God calls mediately by means, which are of two sorts: men and angels. By an angel, He called Philip, a deacon, to be an evangelist. The set or appointed callings in church and commonwealth are ordinarily disposed by men, who are in this matter the instruments of God. Therefore, men lawfully called by them are truly called of God. Thus, the elders of Ephesus, called by the apostles and the rest of the church, are said to be called by the Holy Spirit. And thus we see how God is the author of every calling.

Pursuing Our Calling

I note the final cause, or end, of every calling, in the last words of the description: for the common good, that is, for the benefit and good estate of mankind. In a man's body there are sundry parts and members, and each one has its use and office, which it performs not for itself but for the good of the whole body, as the office of the eye is to see, the ear to hear, and the foot to go. Now, all societies of men are bodies. A family is a body, and so is every church a body, and the commonwealth also. In these bodies there are several members, which are men walking in several callings and offices. Their execution must tend to the happy and good estate of the rest, yea, all men everywhere as much as possible. The common good of men stands in this, not only that they live, but that they live well, in righteousness and holiness, and consequently in true happiness. For the attainment of this, God has ordained and disposed all callings, and in His providence designed the persons to bear them. Here then we must in general know that he abuses his calling, who employs it for himself, seeking wholly his own and not the common good. And that common saying, "every man for himself, and God for us all," is wicked and is directly against the end of every calling or honest kind of life.

32

Holding Faith

Holding faith, and a good conscience.
—1 Timothy 1:19

By "faith," we must understand the wholesome doctrine and religion delivered in the writings of the prophets and apostles.[1] This faith must not go alone but must have its companion, which is "a good conscience," the property of which is to excuse and justify man in all callings before God and man. It is known by a twofold testimony: first, of the past life; second, of the present life and the one to come. The testimony of the past life is that a man has repented of all his past sins and is turned unto God. The testimony of the present life and the life to come is, first, that a man has purposed never to offend God but endeavors to please Him in all things. Second, that when he does slip and sin against God, it is not done wittingly and willingly, but of human infirmity. Third, that a man has his general testimony which is required to a good conscience. "Then shall I not be ashamed, when I have respect unto all thy commandments" (Ps. 119:6). He that breaketh one commandment is guilty of all (see James 2:10)—that is, he who wittingly and willingly,

---

1. *Exposition of Jude*, 90–92.

against the knowledge of his conscience, breaks one of the commandments of God, if occasion is offered, willingly and of knowledge breaks them all. A good conscience must testify on a man's side concerning all sins and all obedience. We have examples in Hezekiah, "Remember now, O LORD,... how I have walked before thee in truth and with a perfect heart" (Isa. 38:3); and in Paul, "I know nothing by myself" (1 Cor. 4:4).

The weight of the ground appears in the following words, where the apostle Paul says that some "put away" good conscience, and concerning the faith "have made shipwreck." Here he compares our conscience to a ship, our religion and faith to our treasure laid in it. As a hole in the ship loses the treasure by sinking the ship, so a crack in the conscience means the treasure of religion suffers shipwreck. It is for this reason that Paul urges Timothy to hold "the mystery of the faith in a pure conscience" (1 Tim. 3:9)....

The first use of this ground is to reveal from God unto man all things needful unto salvation concerning doctrine or manners, wherein it excels all man's learning. First, all the laws and learning of men reveal the moral law only in part, and mingle it with superstitions and ceremonies, but they reveal no part of the gospel. Only this doctrine of faith reveals in full perfection both the law and the gospel. Second, the laws and learning of men know nothing of man's misery, neither the cause nor the remedy thereof. But this doctrine of faith knows and reveals both; namely, the first cause to be the sin of our first parents, and the proper and perfect remedy to be

Holding Faith 135

the death of Christ. Third, men's laws and learning speak at large of temporal happiness but know nothing of eternal. But this doctrine not only knows the true happiness of men but teaches and describes the ready way thereunto.

The second use of this doctrine of faith is that it is a most perfect instrument of the Holy Spirit for the working of all graces in the hearts of men. I mean not the letters and syllables, but the doctrine of the prophets and apostles taught and believed. Paul calls it the "power of God unto salvation" (Rom. 1:16). Christ Himself says that His Word is Spirit and life (John 6:63)—that is, the instrument of the Spirit whereby life eternal is procured. For these two notable uses it is a most precious treasure.

Hence we learn, first, to be "swift to hear" (James 1:19) this doctrine taught in the public ministry, because in it God opens His treasure to dispense the same unto us.

Second, being a precious treasure, we must hide it in the coffers of our hearts: "Thy word have I hid in mine heart" (Ps. 119:11). It must be an "engrafted word" (James 1:21). And this duty we practice (1) when we have care to know it and remember it, and (2) when we set the affections of our hearts upon it, as men do upon their treasures.

Third, if it is the treasure of the church, then it brings to the possessors of it, wealth, honor, and pleasure, as other treasures do. For as the house of Obed-edom was blessed for the ark (2 Sam. 6:11), so is that heart which holds true wisdom within it (Prov. 3:13–14). We in this land have good experience of this truth, who by God's blessing have above forty years enjoyed wealth, peace, honor, and above all, God's protection. And whence have these flowed but from the true faith and religion set down in the prophets and apostles, maintained and defended among us? If we would have this continued, we must also continue to hold and effect this truth as a treasure unto the end.

Reading Perkins

Few men have been as influential in their lifetime as William Perkins, and few men of such fame have been so widely forgotten with the passing of time as Perkins. While living, he published twenty-one books. After his death, these were frequently reprinted. Moreover, friends and students published twenty-seven new books in his name. These were edited from his many manuscripts. John Legate gathered Perkins's works into three volumes in 1608–1609, and these were reprinted more than a dozen times. They were also translated into Latin and published as *Opera Theologica* eight times by 1668. At least fifty editions of Perkins's works were printed in Germany and Switzerland. There were 185 seventeenth-century printings of his individual or collected works in Dutch. Furthermore, his writings were translated into Spanish, Welsh, Irish, French, Italian, Hungarian, and Czech. The international popularity of Perkins's works led one biographer to declare that "his books spoke more tongues than the author ever knew."

Given Perkins's widespread popularity, it is difficult to understand why his works have not been published in English since 1635. It is also a mystery why he was passed over during the renaissance in

Puritan publishing that occurred in the eighteenth century. Thankfully, this oversight has been remedied by the ten-volume publication of Perkins's complete works by Reformation Heritage Books.

Volume 1

Digest or Harmony of the Old and New Testaments
Combat between Christ and the Devil: Matthew 4:1–11
Sermon on the Mount: Matthew 5–7

Volume 2

Commentary on Galatians

Volume 3

Commentary on Hebrews 11

Volume 4

Exposition of Jude
Exposition of Revelation 1–3

Volume 5

Foundation of Christian Religion
Exposition of the Creed
Exposition of the Lord's Prayer

Volume 6

Golden Chain
Manner and Order of Predestination
Treatise on God's Free Grace and Man's Free Will
Fruitful Dialogue Concerning the End of the World
Against Alexander Dickson
On Memory

Volume 7

Reformed Catholic
Problem of the Forged Catholicism
Warning against Idolatry

Volume 8

Discourse on Conscience
Three Books on Cases of Conscience
Treatise Whether a Man Is in Damnation or Grace
A Case of Conscience
Grain of Mustard Seed

Volume 9

True Manner of Knowing Christ Crucified
True Grain
Exhortation to Repentance: Zephaniah 2:1–2
Nature and Practice of Repentance
Combat of the Flesh and Spirit
Man's Imagination
Direction for Government of the Tongue
Damned Art of Witchcraft
Resolution to Countrymen on Prognostication

Volume 10

Treatise on How to Live Well in All Estates
Treatise on Vocations
Right Manner of Erecting and Ordering a Family
Calling of the Ministry
Manner and Method of Preaching
Christian Equity
Treatise on Dying Well

The order of publication is intentional. Volumes 1–4 contain Perkins's exegetical works, volumes 5–7 his doctrinal and polemical works, and volumes 8–10 his practical works. For the reader interested in sampling Perkins's writings, a good place to begin is his sermon series on Christ's Sermon on the Mount or Paul's epistle to the Galatians. These will familiarize you with his exegetical method, theological precision, and pastoral insight. From here, volume 5 is a great introduction to Perkins's theology. He was no innovator but stood in a tradition received from the Reformers and codified in the Church of England's Thirty-Nine Articles. By way of practical works, there are plenty of options, depending in large part on the reader's interest. Perkins's works on the nature of repentance are particularly noteworthy.

For more on Perkins's life, thought, and ministry, see Joel Beeke and Stephen Yuille, *William Perkins*.[1] For a more academic analysis, see William Patterson, *William Perkins and the Making of Protestant England*.[2] For an introduction to Perkins's piety, see Stephen Yuille, *Living Blessedly Forever: The Sermon on the Mount and the Puritan Piety of William Perkins*.[3]

---

1. Joel Beeke and J. Stephen Yuille, *William Perkins*, Bitesize Biographies (Welwyn, Garden City: EP Press, 2015).

2. W. B. Patterson, *William Perkins and the Making of Protestant England* (Oxford: Oxford University Press, 2014).

3. J. Stephen Yuille, *Living Blessedly Forever: The Sermon on the Mount and the Puritan Piety of William Perkins* (Grand Rapids: Reformation Heritage Books, 2012).